MARTIN YAN'S

CHINESE
COOKING

MARTIN YAN'S
INVITATION TO
CHINESE
COOKING

BAY
BOOKS

First published 1999 by Pavilion Books Limited. North
American edition published 2000 by Bay Books, by
arrangement with Pavilion Books.

Bay Books is an imprint of Bay Books & Tapes,
555 De Haro St., No. 220, San Francisco, CA 94107.

Home economy: Allyson Birch
Styling: Helen Lesur
Design: Janet James

For the Bay Books edition:
North American Editor: Cynthia Nims
Proofreader: Ken DellaPenta
Production: Jeff Brandenburg

Library of Congress Cataloging-in-Publication Data:

Yan, Martin, 1948-
        Martin Yan's invitation to Chinese cooking.
                p. cm.
        Originally published: London : Pavilion Books, 1999.
        Includes index.
        ISBN 1-57959-504-9 (hardcover : alk. paper)
        1. Cookery, Chinese. I. Title.

        TX724.5.C5 Y2836 2000
        641.5951—dc21   99-053496

Printed and bound in Singapore

10 9 8 7 6 5 4 3 2 1

Distributed by Publishers Group West

CONTENTS

INTRODUCTION

After five thousand years of evolution, Chinese cooking has finally come of age on the world stage. In a matter of a few short decades, what once was a quiet evolution has become a true revolutionary force of global dimensions. North Americans and Europeans are finally discovering what Chinese and other Asians have known for centuries—that Chinese cooking is delicious, healthy, and easy to prepare once you know how. What's more, it is also great fun!

Today, Chinese cuisine is not only accepted in the West, it is widely praised. We are witnessing a wild and exciting explosion of Chinese restaurants all over the world. I remember a time, and not too long ago, when I was happy to find even a small handful of generic Chinese eateries in my foreign travels. Today I can find a wide array of Sichuan, Hunan, Shanghai, and Cantonese cuisine wherever I go, and some of them in the most unexpected places. I shall never forget visiting England and seeing a sign from a small roadside cafe somewhere in Lancashire. It said, "Fish and Chips, Curry, and Spicy Chinese." The times have certainly changed, and for the better, I might add.

The love of Chinese food is not restricted to fine dining restaurants (or roadside cafes). Home cooks everywhere are now picking up traditional Chinese ingredients and spices and trying them out in their own kitchens. Gone are the days of the weekend roast and potatoes. On Sundays, today's Western families are just as likely to say hello to some oven-baked Chinese roast pork and stir-fried yard-long beans in a peppery garlic sauce.

This book is not intended to be a dust cover for your shelves. It is meant to be a practical guide dedicated to all of you "roll up your sleeves" types who enjoy life through your palates. The recipes in here are for your everyday enjoyment. They are not complicated concoctions that require special equipment and the collective skill of a professional kitchen. Most of the ingredients used in this volume are common and easily available in your local supermarkets. For some of the more specialized items, you many need to pay an occasional visit to Asian grocers. For me, that is not a chore. It is an educational experience.

To make the cooking experience more simple and trouble-free, I have written a chapter outlining some of the basic cooking techniques. To make the text more readable and fun, I have dotted the pages with interesting bits of observation and helpful hints. Chinese cuisine is intricately tied to our culture, so whenever and wherever appropriate I have made comments on Chinese history and social customs.

In the past twenty years, I have had good fortune in bringing Chinese cooking to the West through the *Yan Can Cook* show, my cookbooks, and countless cooking classes and food demonstrations. This book is my special personal invitation to all of you. I would like to share with you many of the wonderful Chinese dishes that I grew up with and the many marvelous recipes that I have collected from my years of travel in great cities throughout North America, Australia, Asia, and Europe. Many of these recipes were inspired by professional Chinese master chefs, but others, equally outstanding, were suggested by homemakers who were blessed with a treasure of family recipes and a keen memory.

In my youth, my mother used to get her children to the dinner table by saying, "Enough talk, let's eat!" Well, enough reading, let's cook! So here's to good food, good taste, and good health!

MARTIN YAN

EVERLASTING

GOOD LUCK

HAPPINESS

JOY

安

PEACE

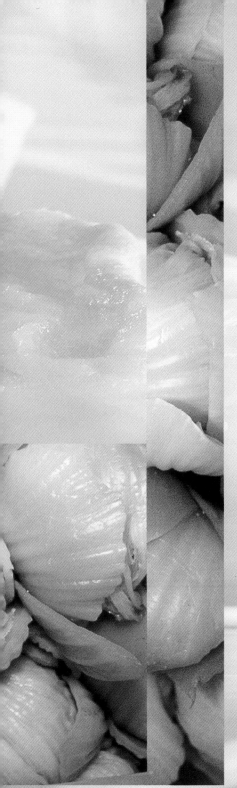

Serving appetizers as a separate first course to a meal is not as common in China as it is in the West. In a typical Chinese family meal, all the courses are served at the same time and shared by everyone around the table. In a formal banquet, the courses are brought to the table one by one, and hot and cold starter dishes are served before the main attractions.

That, however, is not to say that we don't have appetizing small dishes that can delight your guests in a formal gathering or impress a handful of close friends at a casual dinner party. Chinese dim sum dishes are big hits in all settings. At the same time, many of our intricate side dishes can also be served as first courses in a Western-style menu.

Two rules are important when it comes to making appetizers: make ahead and make plenty. Wontons and spring rolls can and should be made ahead of time. This will make your food preparation and cooking time more efficient and enjoyable.

APPETIZERS

CHICKEN IN A PACKET

Not a frozen microwave wonder, these are homemade little bundles of chicken and ham, fresh from the oven and ready to be a contender for the best starter you have ever prepared.

Makes 30

Marinade

2 TABLESPOONS HOISIN SAUCE

2 TABLESPOONS KETCHUP

2 TABLESPOONS CHINESE RICE WINE OR DRY SHERRY

1 TABLESPOON DARK SOY SAUCE

2 TEASPOONS SESAME OIL

1 POUND BONELESS, SKINLESS CHICKEN, CUT INTO 30 BITE-SIZE PIECES

2 OUNCES HAM OR CHINESE SAUSAGE (LOP CHEONG)

2 OUNCES SLICED BAMBOO SHOOTS

6 SLICES GINGER, JULIENNED

2 GREEN ONIONS, JULIENNED

30 CILANTRO LEAVES

30 PIECES FOIL, EACH 5 INCHES SQUARE

Preheat the oven to 400°. Combine the marinade ingredients in a bowl. Add the chicken and stir to coat. Let stand for 15 minutes. Cut the ham into matchstick pieces. If using the Chinese sausage, boil in water for a minute or two before cutting.

On each piece of foil, place one piece of chicken, ham, bamboo shoot, ginger, green onion, and a cilantro leaf. Fold the foil in half to form a triangle. Fold the edges to seal.

Place the packets in a single layer on a baking sheet. Bake until the chicken is opaque when cut, 10 to 12 minutes.

SHRIMP-FILLED MUSHROOMS

Here's the ticket for your next successful cocktail party. Fill your hot appetizer tray with these delicious Shrimp-Filled Mushrooms and get ready for compliments from your guests.

Makes 16

Filling

1 TABLESPOON DRIED SHRIMP

8 OUNCES MEDIUM RAW SHRIMP,
SHELLED, DEVEINED, AND CHOPPED;
OR MINCED PORK

¾ CUP CHOPPED WATER CHESTNUTS

1 TABLESPOON FINELY CHOPPED GINGER

2 TEASPOONS CHOPPED CILANTRO

Marinade

1 EGG WHITE

1 TABLESPOON SOY SAUCE

2 TEASPOONS CHINESE RICE WINE OR
DRY SHERRY

1 TEASPOON CORNSTARCH

½ TEASPOON SALT

¼ TEASPOON SUGAR

¼ TEASPOON WHITE PEPPER

· · ·

8 LARGE WHITE BUTTON MUSHROOMS

8 LARGE FRESH SHIITAKE MUSHROOMS

CORNSTARCH

4 TABLESPOONS COOKING OIL

½ CUP CHICKEN STOCK

Soak the dried shrimp in warm water to cover until softened, about 20 minutes; drain. Chop the dried shrimp and place in a bowl with the raw shrimp or pork, water chestnuts, ginger, and cilantro; mix well. Add the marinade ingredients and mix well. Let stand for 15 minutes.

Discard the stems from the button and shiitake mushrooms. Dust the inside of the mushroom caps with cornstarch; shake to remove excess. Place a tablespoon or two of the filling inside each cap.

Place a wide frying pan over low heat until hot. Add 2 tablespoons oil, swirling to coat the sides. Add half of the mushroom caps, filling side down. Cover and cook until the filling is browned, 5 to 6 minutes. Turn the caps over and add half of the stock. Cover and cook until the caps are tender, about 2 minutes. Place the mushrooms on a warm serving platter while cooking the remaining mushrooms.

Filling Groovy

Filled or stuffed vegetables can make a wonderful side dish or a main dish all by themselves. Try the same filling with peppers, eggplant, and, if you can find them in your Asian market, bitter melons.

CURRY PUFFS

These are my favorite snack from the Chinese bakery. These flaky pastries make a wonderful treat any time of the day. Use prepared pastry and chopped leftover cooked roast or cooked ground beef to make it at home. It is so easy and so good.

Makes 20

Sauce

1 TABLESPOON CHINESE RICE WINE OR
    DRY SHERRY

1 TABLESPOON SOY SAUCE

1 TABLESPOON CURRY POWDER

2 TEASPOONS CHILE GARLIC SAUCE

2 TEASPOONS CORNSTARCH

½ TEASPOON SUGAR

1 TABLESPOON COOKING OIL

⅓ CUP CHOPPED ONION

6 OUNCES COOKED ROAST BEEF, FINELY
    DICED

1 POUND PUFF PASTRY DOUGH

1 EGG YOLK, LIGHTLY BEATEN WITH 1
    TEASPOON WATER

Combine the sauce ingredients in a bowl.

Place a wok or wide frying pan over high heat until hot. Add the oil, swirling to coat the sides. Add the onion; cook, stirring, for about 2 minutes. Add the meat and the sauce and cook, stirring, until the sauce boils and thickens. Remove the filling from the heat and let cool.

Preheat the oven to 375°. On a lightly floured surface, roll out a sheet of dough until ⅛ inch thick. With a cookie cutter, cut the dough into 3-inch rounds.

Place about 2 rounded teaspoons of the filling in the center of each round. Moisten the edges of the dough with water. Fold the dough in half to enclose the filling. Crimp the edges to seal.

Place the turnovers 1 inch apart on a lightly oiled baking sheet. Brush the tops of the turnovers with the egg yolk mixture. Bake until golden brown, 20 to 25 minutes.

CARAMELIZED NUTS

This is my favorite snack to serve friends when they drop by for a visit. The sweet nutty taste goes well with a cup of Chinese green tea, and if my friends stay for dinner, I can use the caramelized nuts in a nice stir-fry dish.

Makes 2 cups

2½ CUPS WALNUTS OR PECANS
1 CUP WATER
¾ CUP SUGAR

3 TABLESPOONS LIGHT CORN SYRUP
COOKING OIL FOR DEEP-FRYING

Skin-Deep Beauty

When nuts are parboiled, tannins in the skin are eliminated, which eliminates the nuts' natural bitterness. Skinless walnuts, peanuts, and almonds are also available in Asian groceries and some specialty supermarkets.

Bring a pot of water to a boil. Add the nuts and blanch for 2 minutes; drain.

Combine the water, sugar, and corn syrup in a pan. Cook, stirring, over medium heat until the sugar dissolves. Add the nuts and simmer, stirring occasionally, until the syrup reaches 220° on a sugar thermometer. (At this point, the syrup runs off a cool metal spoon in two drops that merge to form a sheet.) Immediately drain the nuts in a metal colander or sieve, then spread on a lightly oiled baking sheet. Let cool completely.

In a wok, heat the oil for deep-frying to 275°. Add the nuts and deep-fry, stirring often to prevent sticking, for 5 minutes. Gradually increase the heat to 300°. Continue cooking until the nuts turn golden brown, 1 to 2 minutes.

Place the nuts on a foil-lined baking sheet to cool completely. Store the nuts in an airtight container in the refrigerator.

HOISIN-GLAZED CHAR SIU

The Cantonese word for barbecued pork baked in an oven is char, *but it definitely does not mean burnt. Follow the recipe, and the wonderful aroma of pork baking in your oven will soon fill your entire house.*

Makes 4 to 6 servings

Marinade

½ CUP HOISIN SAUCE OR CHAR SIU SAUCE

3 TABLESPOONS CHINESE RICE WINE OR DRY SHERRY

3 TABLESPOONS SOY SAUCE

1 TABLESPOON FINELY CHOPPED GINGER

1 TABLESPOON FINELY CHOPPED GARLIC

◆ ◆ ◆

2 POUNDS BONELESS PORK BUTT

HOISIN SAUCE OR CHAR SIU SAUCE

Cut the pork into ½-inch-thick slices. Combine the marinade ingredients in a large bowl or pan. Add the pork and turn to coat. Cover and refrigerate for 4 hours or overnight.

Preheat the oven to 350°. Arrange the pork in a single layer on a rack over a large foil-lined baking sheet. Bake for 30 minutes. Turn the slices over and baste with the hoisin sauce. Continue baking until tender, 20 to 30 minutes, brushing occasionally with the hoisin sauce.

A Sauce by Any Name

Hoisin in Chinese actually means "fresh seafood," but hoisin sauce is best known as a condiment for Peking Duck and Mu Shu Pork. It is made from fermented soybean paste, vinegar, garlic, sugar, and a touch of five-spice powder and chiles. It makes a versatile marinade and basting sauce for many grilled or roasted meats. It can also be used to season a variety of stir-fry meat dishes.

SHANGHAI SPRING ROLLS

Early Chinese immigrants to North America created a larger version of the traditional Chinese spring roll and called it an egg roll. Spring rolls were originally a Shanghai specialty, served during Chinese New Year celebrations as a special tribute to the beginning of spring.

Makes 40

Filling

2 DRIED BLACK (SHIITAKE) MUSHROOMS

2 OUNCES DRIED BEAN THREAD
   NOODLES

8 OUNCES GROUND LEAN PORK

4 OUNCES MEDIUM RAW SHRIMP,
   SHELLED, DEVEINED, AND CHOPPED

3 TABLESPOONS COARSELY CHOPPED
   ONION

2 TABLESPOONS JULIENNED CARROT

1 TABLESPOON CHINESE RICE WINE OR
   DRY SHERRY

2 TEASPOONS SOY SAUCE

1 TEASPOON SESAME OIL

¾ TEASPOON SUGAR

¼ TEASPOON SALT

◆ ◆ ◆

40 SPRING ROLL WRAPPERS, 4 INCHES
   SQUARE

COOKING OIL FOR DEEP-FRYING

Soak the mushrooms in warm water to cover until softened, about 15 minutes; drain. Discard the stems and thinly slice the caps.

Soak the bean thread noodles in warm water to cover until softened, about 15 minutes; drain. Bring a pot of water to a boil. Add the noodles and cook until they turn translucent, about 2 minutes. Drain, rinse with cold running water, and drain again. Cut the noodles into 2- to 3-inch lengths.

Place the mushrooms and noodles in a bowl. Add the remaining filling ingredients and mix well. Let stand for 15 minutes.

Place a teaspoon or two of the filling diagonally across the center of a wrapper. Moisten the edges of the wrapper with water. Fold the bottom edge over the filling, then fold in the sides. Roll up to form a tight cylinder. Repeat with the remaining filling and wrappers.

In a wok, heat the oil for deep-frying to 350°. Deep-fry the spring rolls, a few at a time, turning occasionally, until golden brown, 2 to 3 minutes. Remove and drain on paper towels. Keep warm in a 200° oven while cooking the remaining spring rolls.

RIGHT SHANGHAI SPRING ROLLS, CANTONESE SHRIMP TOAST, AND GOLDEN CRAB TRIANGLES

FIVE-FLAVOR HONEY WINGS

The recipe is for eight wings, but I suggest that you double the recipe.
These sweet wings will fly off your serving platter in no time.

Makes about 16

8 WHOLE CHICKEN WINGS

2 TABLESPOONS OYSTER SAUCE

1 TABLESPOON CORNSTARCH

1 TABLESPOON COOKING OIL

1 GREEN ONION, SLICED

2 TABLESPOONS FINELY CHOPPED GARLIC

1 TEASPOON DRIED RED PEPPER FLAKES

¾ CUP CHICKEN STOCK

2 TABLESPOONS DARK SOY SAUCE

2 TABLESPOONS CHINESE RICE WINE OR
   DRY SHERRY

½ TEASPOON CHINESE FIVE-SPICE
   POWDER

2 TABLESPOONS HONEY

Separate the chicken wings into sections; reserve the bony tips for other
uses or discard. Combine the oyster sauce and cornstarch in a bowl. Add
the chicken and stir to coat. Let stand for 15 minutes.

Place a wok or wide frying pan over high heat until hot. Add the oil,
swirling to coat the sides. Add the chicken and cook, turning several times,
until golden brown, about 3 minutes. Add the green onion, garlic, and
pepper flakes; cook, stirring, until fragrant, about 10 seconds. Add the
chicken stock, soy sauce, rice wine, and five-spice powder; bring to a boil.
Reduce the heat to low, cover, and simmer until the chicken is tender when
pierced, about 12 minutes.

Increase the heat to high. Add the honey and cook until the chicken is
well glazed.

VEGETABLE BASKET WITH CHILE AND PEANUT TOFU DIPS

Need a break from the same old blue cheese or French onion dip? Take the exotic route and serve up a platter of vegetables with these two tofu-based dips.

Makes about 10 to 14 fluid ounces (each recipe)

Chile Tofu Dip	*Peanut Tofu Dip*
14 OUNCES SOFT TOFU, DRAINED	7 OUNCES SOFT TOFU, DRAINED
½ CUP MAYONNAISE	¼ CUP CHUNKY PEANUT BUTTER
2 TABLESPOONS CHILE GARLIC SAUCE	¼ CUP UNSWEETENED COCONUT MILK
1 TABLESPOON SOY SAUCE	1 GREEN ONION, CHOPPED
1 TABLESPOON WORCESTERSHIRE SAUCE	1 TABLESPOON SUGAR
1 TABLESPOON SESAME OIL	1 TABLESPOON CHILE GARLIC SAUCE
	2 TEASPOONS DARK SOY SAUCE
	2 TEASPOONS CHOPPED GARLIC

To make each dip, place all of its ingredients in a blender or food processor and process until smooth. Place each dip in a separate bowl.

Serve with a platter of assorted raw vegetables, such as bok choy, broccoli, cauliflower, daikon, snow peas, red and green bell peppers, sugar snap peas, or your own choices.

Mandarin Pan-Fried Dumplings

In Northern China, Mandarin pan-fried dumplings, also called potstickers, are served in the morning for breakfast and in the afternoon as snacks. They are one of Beijing's most popular street foods.

Makes 28

Filling

5 OUNCES NAPA CABBAGE, SLICED

1 TEASPOON SALT

8 OUNCES GROUND LEAN PORK

1 CUP CHOPPED CARROT

¼ CUP CHOPPED WATER CHESTNUTS

2 GREEN ONIONS, CHOPPED

1½ TABLESPOONS OYSTER SAUCE

1 TABLESPOON CHINESE RICE WINE OR
    DRY SHERRY

1 TABLESPOON CORNSTARCH

2 TEASPOONS SESAME OIL

1 TEASPOON FINELY CHOPPED GINGER

½ TEASPOON SUGAR

◦ ◦ ◦

28 POTSTICKER WRAPPERS

3 TABLESPOONS COOKING OIL

⅔ CUP CHICKEN STOCK

CHILE OIL

RICE VINEGAR

SOY SAUCE

Combine the cabbage and salt in a bowl; mix well. Let stand for 10 minutes. Squeeze to extract the excess liquid; discard the liquid.

Add the remaining filling ingredients; mix well. Let stand for 15 minutes.

To make each dumpling, place a heaped teaspoon of filling in the center of a wrapper. Moisten the edges of the wrapper with water. Fold the wrapper in half, crimping one side, to form a semicircle. Set the dumplings on a baking sheet, seam side up, so they sit flat. Cover the dumplings with a towel while filling the remaining wrappers.

Place a wide frying pan over medium heat until hot. Add 1½ tablespoons of the oil, swirling to coat the sides. Add the dumplings, half at a time, seam side up. Cook until the bottoms are golden brown, 3 to 4 minutes. Add ⅓ cup stock. Reduce the heat to low; cover and cook until the liquid is absorbed, 5 to 6 minutes. Cook the remaining dumplings with the remaining oil and stock.

Place the dumplings, browned side up, on a serving platter with chile oil, rice vinegar, and soy sauce on the side.

Sticking to the Pot
Potstickers are so named because of the way their bottoms are browned in the pot before broth or water is added for pan-steaming. I find this potsticking technique quite a useful one. You can use the same process on steamed buns or *siu mai* (open-topped dumplings filled with ground shrimp and pork).

GOLDEN CRAB TRIANGLES

Throughout my travels in North America, I often find this delightful appetizer listed on the menu as Seafood Wontons. You can make these the easy way by folding them into triangles.

Makes 30

Filling

1 TEASPOON COOKING OIL

¼ CUP FINELY CHOPPED ONION

5 OUNCES COOKED CRABMEAT, FLAKED

3 TABLESPOONS FINELY GRATED CARROT

1 GREEN ONION, FINELY CHOPPED

2 TEASPOONS FISH SAUCE

1 TEASPOON FINELY CHOPPED GINGER

1 TEASPOON OYSTER SAUCE

⅛ TEASPOON WHITE PEPPER

• • •

30 WONTON WRAPPERS

COOKING OIL FOR DEEP-FRYING

To make the filling, place a small frying pan over medium heat until hot. Add the oil, swirling to coat the sides. Add the onion; stir-fry for 1½ minutes. Place in a bowl with the remaining filling ingredients; mix well.

To make each triangle, place a heaped teaspoon of the filling diagonally across the center of a wonton wrapper. Moisten the edges of the wrapper with water. Fold over the filling to form a triangle.

In a wok, heat the oil for deep-frying to 350°. Deep-fry the triangles, a few at a time, turning occasionally, until golden brown, about 1 minute. Remove and drain on paper towels.

CANTONESE SHRIMP TOAST

Aside from being an appetizing dim sum treat, shrimp toast is the best way I can think of to give new life to day-old bread.

Makes 24

12 SLICES DAY-OLD WHITE BREAD

Shrimp Paste

8 OUNCES MEDIUM RAW SHRIMP,
   SHELLED AND DEVEINED

¼ CUP FINELY CHOPPED CARROT

1 EGG WHITE

2 TEASPOONS CORNSTARCH

2 TEASPOONS CHINESE RICE WINE OR
   DRY SHERRY

½ TEASPOON FINELY CHOPPED GARLIC

½ TEASPOON SALT

⅛ TEASPOON WHITE PEPPER

1 TEASPOON CORIANDER SEED

12 MEDIUM RAW SHRIMP, SHELLED,
   DEVEINED, AND CUT IN HALF
   HORIZONTALLY

COOKING OIL FOR DEEP-FRYING

Cut off and discard the bread crusts, then cut each bread slice in half diagonally to form two triangles.

Place the shrimp, carrot, egg white, cornstarch, rice wine, garlic, salt, and pepper in a food processor; process until the mixture forms a chunky paste. Place in a bowl and add the coriander seed; mix well.

Spread the shrimp paste about ¼ inch thick on one side of each bread triangle. Place 1 shrimp half on each bread triangle, pressing it firmly into the shrimp paste.

In a wok, heat the oil for deep-frying to 325°. Deep-fry the bread triangles, a few at a time, until golden brown, 1½ to 2 minutes on each side. Remove and drain on paper towels.

Have a Ball

Looking for new ways to use shrimp paste? Make a batch and add a little extra cornstarch to the mix. Shape the paste into balls and steam them on a heatproof dish in a wok. Ten minutes should be sufficient for 10 balls. If you have a pot of broth, have a ball and throw in a dozen shrimp balls for 4 servings.

NEW ASIA ROLL-UPS

The "wrap" is a recent food craze in the West, but in China we have been wrapping our food for hundreds of years. This is a great party dish that allows everyone to create his or her own dinner. Let's rock and roll!

Makes 8

Dipping Sauce

3 TABLESPOONS SEASONED RICE
  VINEGAR

2 TABLESPOONS FISH SAUCE

2 TABLESPOONS FRESHLY SQUEEZED
  LIME JUICE

2 TEASPOONS CHILE SAUCE

2 TABLESPOONS SUGAR

1 TEASPOON FINELY CHOPPED GARLIC

8 OUNCES BONELESS, SKINLESS
  CHICKEN THIGHS

3 TABLESPOONS STORE-BOUGHT
  CHICKEN MARINADE

1 GREEN ONION, CHOPPED

2 TABLESPOONS COOKING OIL

1/2 RED BELL PEPPER, SEEDED AND
  JULIENNED

4 OUNCES ENOKI MUSHROOMS, ENDS
  TRIMMED

1 1/2 CUPS WATERCRESS LEAVES

1 1/2 CUPS CILANTRO LEAVES

2 OUNCES CHOPPED CARAMELIZED NUTS
  (SEE PAGE 18)

8 LETTUCE LEAVES

Combine dipping sauce ingredients in a bowl. Combine the chicken, marinade, and green onion in a bowl; turn to coat. Let stand for 15 minutes.

Place a wide frying pan over high heat until hot. Add the oil, swirling to coat the sides. Add the chicken and pan-fry until the chicken is no longer pink when cut, 2 to 3 minutes on each side. Let cool slightly, then shred.

To eat, place some chicken, bell pepper, mushrooms, watercress, cilantro, and nuts in a lettuce leaf. Wrap up and eat out of your hands, dipping the roll-up in the sauce.

SESAME- AND ALMOND-COATED SCALLOPS

This is elegance made easy. The scallops take only a couple of minutes to pan-fry, and the sweet and sour sauce brings to this dish a touch of excitement and sophistication.

Makes 4 to 6 appetizer servings

Marinade

1 TABLESPOON CHINESE RICE WINE OR
   DRY SHERRY
2 TEASPOONS CORNSTARCH
½ TEASPOON SALT
¼ TEASPOON WHITE PEPPER

◆ ◆ ◆

12 OUNCES SEA SCALLOPS

Dipping Sauce

½ CUP SWEET AND SOUR SAUCE
4 TEASPOONS WATER
4 TEASPOONS MUSTARD POWDER
1 TABLESPOON SOY SAUCE

◆ ◆ ◆

½ CUP FINELY CHOPPED ALMONDS
¼ CUP WHITE SESAME SEEDS
½ TEASPOON CHINESE FIVE-SPICE
   POWDER
CORNSTARCH
1 EGG, LIGHTLY BEATEN
¼ CUP COOKING OIL

Combine the marinade ingredients in a bowl. Add the scallops and mix well. Let stand for 15 minutes. Combine the dipping sauce ingredients in a bowl.

In a bowl, combine the almonds, sesame seeds, and five-spice powder. Lightly dust the scallops with cornstarch; shake to remove excess. Dip in the egg, drain briefly, then coat with the almond mixture.

Place a wide frying pan over medium heat until hot. Add the oil, swirling to coat the sides. Add the scallops and pan-fry, turning once, until golden brown, about 2 minutes on each side. Place on a serving platter and serve with the dipping sauce on the side.

WONDERFUL WONTONS

Wonton in Chinese literally means "swallowing the cloud." What a picturesque way to describe the light and fluffy meat-filled dumplings that are often served in a savory broth or, as in this recipe, by themselves with a dipping sauce.

Makes 24

Filling

4 OUNCES GROUND LEAN MEAT

4 OUNCES MEDIUM RAW SHRIMP, SHELLED, DEVEINED, AND CHOPPED

2 OUNCES BAMBOO SHOOTS, FINELY CHOPPED

1 GREEN ONION, CHOPPED

2 TABLESPOONS CHINESE RICE WINE OR DRY SHERRY

1 TABLESPOON OYSTER SAUCE

2 TEASPOONS CORNSTARCH

1/4 TEASPOON WHITE PEPPER

♦ ♦ ♦

24 WONTON WRAPPERS

COOKING OIL FOR DEEP-FRYING

SWEET AND SOUR SAUCE

Combine the filling ingredients in a bowl; mix well. Let stand for 15 minutes.

Place a heaped teaspoon of the filling in the center of a wonton wrapper. Moisten the edges of the wrapper with water. Fold the wrapper in half over the filling to form a triangle. Pinch the edges to seal. Pull the two opposite corners together, moisten one corner, and overlap with the other corner; press to seal. Cover the dumplings with a towel while filling the remaining wrappers.

In a wok, heat the oil for deep-frying to 350°. Deep-fry the wontons, half at a time, turning frequently, until golden brown, 2 to 3 minutes. Drain on paper towels.

Arrange on a serving platter with the sweet and sour sauce for dipping.

Wrap Artist

Wonton wrappers are made from wheat flour, water, and eggs. These small, flat squares come in two thicknesses. The thicker ones are for wontons that will be deep-fried, pan-fried, and steamed. The thinner ones are better for wontons served in broth.

A good bowl of soup is the most popular way to start any Chinese meal. Compared to their Western cousins, Chinese soups are generally lighter, and they are not served separately as a first course but alongside other dishes, to be enjoyed throughout the meal. A good soup quenches your thirst and cleanses your palate.

The secret to any good soup is a good chicken or vegetable stock. In this chapter, I have listed a couple of trusted and well-tested stock recipes. My golden rule on stock making is simply this: make extra! You can always freeze it and use it later. It certainly will save you time and a trip to the supermarket.

Finally, a great soup does not take hours to prepare. The recipes in this chapter are quick and easy, designed to suit today's busy lifestyles.

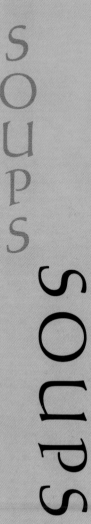

SOUPS

CHINESE CHEF'S CHICKEN STOCK

A good, rich chicken stock is more than just a base for soup. It adds flavor to Chinese stir-fried dishes without compromising or overwhelming the spices.

Makes 2 quarts

2 QUARTS COLD WATER

2½ POUNDS RAW CHICKEN BONES

8 OUNCES LEAN PORK

8 OUNCES HAM HOCK (OPTIONAL)

3 GREEN ONIONS, CUT IN HALF

6 SLICES GINGER, LIGHTLY CRUSHED

⅛ TEASPOON WHITE PEPPER

SALT

In a large pot, bring the water, chicken bones, pork, and ham hock to a boil. Skim off any foam that forms on the top. Reduce the heat to low, cover, and simmer for 1½ hours. Add the green onions, ginger, and pepper; simmer for 30 minutes. Skim and discard the fat from the stock. Take out the pork, slice, and serve as a side dish with soy sauce. Strain the stock; discard the solids. Add salt to taste when ready to use.

Note: **For more flavor, you can also add star anise.**

To Make Chicken Soup
Add chicken meat to hot stock, and increase the amount of ginger and green onions.

CHINESE CHEF'S VEGETABLE STOCK

This recipe is perfect for vegetarians as well as those of us who fancy a light yet flavorful stock. It's versatile and can be used in stir-fried and braised dishes, and, of course, it's a fantastic base for soup. Don't worry about making too much; freeze the extra for later use.

Makes 2 quarts

½ TEASPOON SICHUAN PEPPERCORNS

1 TABLESPOON COOKING OIL

1 ONION, SLICED

6 SLICES GINGER, LIGHTLY CRUSHED

3 CLOVES GARLIC, LIGHTLY CRUSHED

3 GREEN ONIONS, SLICED

2 QUARTS COLD WATER

3 CARROTS, SLICED

1 STALK CELERY, SLICED

3 SPRIGS CILANTRO (OPTIONAL)

2 TABLESPOONS SOY SAUCE

½ POD STAR ANISE (OPTIONAL)

SALT AND PEPPER

Seasoning Your Stock
Remember to salt your stock at the end of the cooking process. If you add salt too early, it will be concentrated when the stock reduces during the cooking process, and you will end up with a stock that is too salty.

Place the peppercorns in a small frying pan over medium heat. Cook, shaking the pan frequently, until the peppercorns darken slightly and smell toasted, 3 to 4 minutes.

Place a pot over medium heat until hot. Add the oil, swirling to coat the sides. Add the onion, ginger, garlic, and green onions; cook, stirring, for 2 minutes. Add the water, carrots, celery, cilantro, soy sauce, star anise, and toasted peppercorns; bring to a boil. Reduce the heat, cover, and simmer for 1½ hours. Strain the stock; discard the solids. Add salt and pepper to taste when ready to use.

FISH AND SPINACH SOUP

This is an old family recipe that I improved upon when I moved to North America. In addition to spinach, I added some frozen mixed vegetables, which are convenient and go well with any kind of white fish.

Makes 4 to 6 servings

½ TEASPOON SICHUAN PEPPERCORNS

1 QUART CHICKEN STOCK

2 CUPS WATER

2 TABLESPOONS CHINESE RICE WINE OR
   DRY SHERRY

2 TABLESPOONS SOY SAUCE

14 OUNCES SOFT OR REGULAR TOFU,
   DRAINED AND DICED

8 OUNCES FIRM WHITE FISH FILLETS,
   CUT INTO BITE-SIZE PIECES

4 OUNCES FROZEN MIXED VEGETABLES,
   SUCH AS PEAS AND CARROTS, THAWED

8 OUNCES SPINACH LEAVES, WASHED
   AND TRIMMED

Place the peppercorns in a small frying pan over medium heat. Cook, shaking the pan frequently, until the peppercorns darken slightly and smell toasted, about 3 to 4 minutes. Grind in a spice grinder until coarsely ground.

In a large pot, combine the stock, water, rice wine, soy sauce, and ground peppercorns. Bring to a boil over medium-high heat. Add the tofu, fish, and mixed vegetables; reduce the heat to low and simmer until the fish turns opaque, about 5 minutes. Add the spinach and cook for 1 minute.

OXTAIL SOUP

Because oxtails have a rich, meaty flavor and texture, they make fantastic soup. Add dried tangerine peel, star anise, cloves, and fennel seeds, and you will soon have yourself a rich, tasty, and nourishing treat that is perfect for those nippy winter nights.

Makes 4 to 6 servings

1 PIECE DRIED TANGERINE PEEL

2 WHOLE STAR ANISE

1/2 TEASPOON WHOLE CLOVES

1/2 TEASPOON FENNEL SEEDS

1 TABLESPOON COOKING OIL

2 POUNDS OXTAIL, CUT INTO SECTIONS

4 CLOVES GARLIC, FINELY CHOPPED

2 SLICES GINGER, FINELY CHOPPED

1 QUART BEEF STOCK

1 QUART COLD WATER

1/4 CUP CHINESE RICE WINE OR DRY SHERRY

3 TABLESPOONS SOY SAUCE

1 TABLESPOON HOISIN SAUCE

2 TEASPOONS SUGAR

14 OUNCES DAIKON, SPLIT LENGTHWISE, THEN CUT INTO CHUNKS

2 CARROTS, SLICED

2 GREEN ONIONS, CUT INTO 2-INCH PIECES

1/2 TEASPOON SESAME OIL

Soak the tangerine peel in warm water to cover until softened, about 30 minutes; drain. Tie up the tangerine peel, star anise, cloves, and fennel seeds in a piece of cheesecloth.

Place a large pot over high heat until hot. Add the oil, swirling to coat the sides. Add the oxtail and cook until lightly browned on all sides, about 10 minutes. Add the garlic and ginger; cook, stirring, until fragrant, about 10 seconds. Add the spice bag, stock, water, rice wine, soy sauce, hoisin sauce, and sugar; bring to a boil. Reduce the heat to low; cover and simmer until the oxtail is tender, about 2 1/2 hours.

Add the daikon and carrots; cook until the vegetables are tender, 15 to 20 minutes. Discard the spice bag. Add the green onions and cook for 2 minutes. Stir in the sesame oil.

Tangerine Peel

Don't worry if you don't grow tangerines in your garden. Dried tangerine peel is available in Asian grocery shops, usually in cellophane packages. Soak the peel briefly to soften it up before using. It has a sweet citrus smell and pungent flavor. If you can't find tangerine peel, substitute fresh orange zest.

SINGING RICE AND SEAFOOD SOUP

Great Chinese food must look good, smell good, and taste good. In the case of this soup, I need to add that it must also sound good. Singing Rice and Seafood Soup is a spectacular treat any time, and especially when you are entertaining guests at home. Just watch their faces when the rice crusts sizzle and crackle in their bowls. If fish balls aren't available, use firm white fish fillets cut into bite-size cubes.

Makes 6 to 8 servings

Marinade

1 TABLESPOON CHINESE RICE WINE OR
    DRY SHERRY

1 TEASPOON CORNSTARCH

◆ ◆ ◆

4 OUNCES RAW SHRIMP, SHELLED,
    DEVEINED, AND CUT INTO BITE-SIZE
    PIECES

4 OUNCES SCALLOPS, CUT INTO BITE-
    SIZE PIECES

1½ QUARTS CHICKEN STOCK

3 SLICES GINGER, LIGHTLY CRUSHED

8 OUNCES FROZEN FISH BALLS, THAWED
    AND CUT IN HALF

2 OUNCES STRAW MUSHROOMS,
    CUT IN HALF

1 CARROT, SLICED

1 ZUCCHINI, SLICED

4 GREEN ONIONS, SLICED

¼ CUP SOY SAUCE

3 TABLESPOONS CHINESE RICE WINE OR
    DRY SHERRY

1 TEASPOON SESAME OIL

½ TEASPOON WHITE PEPPER

COOKING OIL FOR DEEP-FRYING

8 RICE CRUSTS, EACH 2 INCHES SQUARE
    (SEE RIGHT)

Combine the marinade ingredients in a bowl. Add the shrimp and scallops; stir to coat. Let stand for 10 minutes.

In a large pot, bring the stock and ginger to a boil over medium-high heat. Add the shrimp, scallops, fish balls, and straw mushrooms. Reduce the heat to low; cover and simmer for 2 minutes. Add the carrot and zucchini; simmer for 4 minutes. Add the green onions, soy sauce, rice wine, sesame oil, and pepper. Cook, stirring occasionally, for 2 minutes. Discard the ginger slices.

In a wok, heat the oil to 375°. Deep-fry the rice crusts, one half at a time and turning continuously, until puffed and golden, 15 to 20 seconds. Remove and drain on paper towels.

To serve, bring the soup to the table in a tureen. Slide the hot rice crusts into the hot soup and listen to the sizzle. Break the rice crusts with the ladle and serve.

Making Rice Crust

In the old days, getting rice crust was only a matter of scraping it off the bottom of the rice pot. Today's electric rice cookers make such an option obsolete. Not to worry. Spread cooked rice in a thin layer inside a greased, shallow baking pan. Cut into squares with a wet knife. Bake in a 350° oven until the rice squares are firm and dry, about 50 minutes. Store rice crusts in an airtight container at room temperature.

ROAST DUCK SOUP WITH BEAN THREAD NOODLES

Chinese chefs are firm believers in the saying, "Waste not, want not." Nothing goes to waste. The carcass of a roast duck makes a wonderful broth when you drop in a few slices of ginger and green onion. What about the rest of the duck? Well, there's shredded duck breast in a salad and then roast duck for a dinner entrée. One duck for three dishes: the rewards of economizing!

Makes 4 servings

2 DRIED BLACK (SHIITAKE) MUSHROOMS

2 OUNCES DRIED BEAN THREAD NOODLES (OPTIONAL)

2 QUARTS COLD WATER

1 ROAST DUCK CARCASS, EXCESS FAT REMOVED

2 SLICES GINGER, LIGHTLY CRUSHED

4 GREEN ONIONS, CUT INTO 2-INCH PIECES

1 CARROT, JULIENNED

2 CUPS SLICED NAPA CABBAGE

¾ CUP SLICED WATER CHESTNUTS

8 OUNCES CHINESE ROAST DUCK BREAST, THINLY SLICED

2 TABLESPOONS SOY SAUCE

Soak the mushrooms in warm water to cover until softened, about 15 minutes; drain. Discard the stems and thinly slice the caps. Soak the bean thread noodles in warm water to cover until softened, about 5 minutes; drain. Cut the noodles into 4-inch lengths.

In a large pot, bring the water to a boil over medium-high heat. Add the duck carcass, ginger, and half of the green onions; bring to a boil. Reduce the heat to low, cover, and simmer for 1 hour. Strain and discard the solids; skim and discard the fat.

Place 1 quart of the duck stock in a pot. Reserve the rest for another use. Add the mushrooms, noodles, carrot, cabbage, and water chestnuts; cook until the cabbage is tender, 4 to 5 minutes. Add the remaining green onions, the duck meat, and soy sauce; cook until heated through.

Buying a Roast Duck

Thanks to the recent wave of immigrants, Chinese roast ducks are no longer a rare find in Western countries. Take a walk through Chinatown, and you will come across many delicatessens and restaurants where roast ducks are displayed proudly in the windows. Don't be put off by the sight of their heads—the seller can remove them!

CORN AND CRAB SOUP

Corn soup originated in the West, but it was adopted by the Chinese with great fondness, and over the years it has become a popular item on our menus. I've added crab and scallops to this recipe, although you may also experiment with shrimp or other seafood.

Makes 4 to 6 servings

4 DRIED BLACK (SHIITAKE) MUSHROOMS

1½ QUARTS CHICKEN STOCK

1 SLICE GINGER, JULIENNED

1-POUND CAN CREAM-STYLE CORN

4 OUNCES SCALLOPS, QUARTERED IF LARGE

4 OUNCES COOKED CRABMEAT, FLAKED

1 TEASPOON SESAME OIL

½ TEASPOON SALT

¼ TEASPOON WHITE PEPPER

¼ CUP CORNSTARCH DISSOLVED IN ¼ CUP WATER

1 EGG, LIGHTLY BEATEN

CHOPPED GREEN ONIONS

Soak the mushrooms in warm water to cover until softened, about 15 minutes; reserve the mushroom soaking liquid. Discard the stems and thinly slice the caps.

In a large pot, bring the stock, reserved mushroom soaking liquid, and ginger to a boil over medium-high heat. Add the mushrooms, corn, scallops, and crabmeat; cook until the scallops turn opaque, about 1 minute. Stir in the sesame oil, salt, and pepper. Add the cornstarch mixture and cook, stirring, until the soup boils and thickens slightly.

Remove the soup from the heat and slowly drizzle in the egg, stirring in one direction until the egg forms short threads. Garnish with the green onions and serve immediately.

Note: **In place of the cream-style corn, you could instead use 8 ounces fresh or frozen corn puréed, with a ladle or two of the stock, in a blender.**

SEAFOOD EGG FLOWER SOUP

Egg Flower Soup is a classic in all overseas Chinese restaurants. Just to prove that one can always improve on a classic, I've added shrimp and scallops to this recipe. Use my suggested ingredients as a guide, or, if you wish, experiment with other fresh seafood that is in season. Remember, the best ingredient that you can add to any dish is your imagination.

Makes 4 to 6 servings

Marinade

½ TEASPOON CORNSTARCH

¼ TEASPOON SALT

¼ TEASPOON WHITE PEPPER

• • •

4 OUNCES SCALLOPS, QUARTERED IF
    LARGE

2 OUNCES SMALL RAW SHRIMP, SHELLED
    AND DEVEINED

Seasonings

2½ TABLESPOONS CORNSTARCH
    DISSOLVED IN 3 TABLESPOONS WATER

2 TEASPOONS SOY SAUCE

1 TEASPOON SESAME OIL

• • •

1 TABLESPOON COOKING OIL

2 SLICES GINGER, JULIENNED

1 QUART CHICKEN STOCK

5 OUNCES SOFT TOFU, DRAINED AND
    CUT INTO CUBES

1 TOMATO, SEEDED AND DICED

3 OUNCES STRAW MUSHROOMS

2 TABLESPOONS SHANGHAI PICKLED
    VEGETABLE, RINSED AND CHOPPED
    (OPTIONAL)

2 TABLESPOONS FROZEN PEAS, THAWED

2 GREEN ONIONS, SLICED

1 EGG, LIGHTLY BEATEN

Egg Flower

This is one flower that you can't grow in your garden. Instead of a green thumb, you need a steady hand. Drizzle eggs slowly into the soup, and stir evenly; the eggs should cook in thin ribbons.

Combine the marinade ingredients in a bowl. Add the scallops and shrimp; stir to coat. Let stand for 10 minutes. Combine the seasoning ingredients in a bowl.

Place a large pot over medium heat until hot. Add the oil, swirling to coat the sides. Add the ginger and cook, stirring, until fragrant, about 10 seconds. Add the scallops and shrimp; stir-fry for 1 minute. Add the stock, tofu, tomato, mushrooms, pickled vegetable, peas, and green onions; bring to a boil. Add the seasonings and cook, stirring, until the soup boils and thickens slightly.

Remove the soup from the heat and slowly drizzle in the egg, stirring in one direction until the egg forms short threads. Serve immediately.

TOMATO SOUP WITH SHRIMP AND OMELET STRIPS

On my first visit to Britain, I was treated to a simple but absolutely wonderful bowl of tomato soup. It was one of the most vivid memories of my stay. Here's a recipe that gives it a Chinese touch. I hope it will create a fond memory for you.

Makes 4 servings

2 EGGS

2 GREEN ONIONS, FINELY CHOPPED

1/8 TEASPOON SALT

2 TEASPOONS COOKING OIL

1 QUART CHICKEN STOCK

2 TEASPOONS SOY SAUCE

8 OUNCES TOMATOES, PEELED, SEEDED, AND CUT INTO 1-INCH PIECES

8 OUNCES SMALL RAW SHRIMP, SHELLED AND DEVEINED

7 OUNCES SOFT TOFU, DRAINED AND CUT INTO 1/2-INCH CUBES

1/2 TEASPOON SESAME OIL

SLICED GREEN ONION

Combine the eggs, chopped green onions, and salt in a bowl; whisk to combine.

Place a 8- to 9-inch nonstick omelet pan over medium heat until hot. Add the oil, swirling to coat the sides. Add the egg mixture and cook without stirring. As the edges begin to set, lift with a spatula and shake or tilt to let the egg flow underneath. When the egg no longer flows freely, turn over and cook 5 seconds. Slide the omelet onto a cutting board. Cut into thin strips, about 1/4 inch wide.

In a large pot, bring the stock and soy sauce to a boil over medium heat. Add the tomatoes, reduce the heat to low, cover, and simmer for 5 minutes. Add the shrimp and tofu; cook until the shrimp turn opaque, about 2 minutes. Stir in the sesame oil.

Pour the soup into individual bowls and garnish with the sliced green onion and omelet strips. Serve immediately.

British Food

I must have heard every single joke about British food before I ever set foot in the British Isles, so imagine my surprise when I discovered a vibrant and innovative culinary scene. Today's British chefs are well schooled, imaginative, and not at all shy about adapting international flavors and cooking techniques. In addition to being wizards of Indian spices, many of them have also discovered the joys of ginger, fermented black beans, and even pressed tofu. I was especially delighted to see a touch of the East in many of their creations.

WEST LAKE BEEF WITH SEAWEED IN SAVORY BROTH

Marco Polo visited Hangzhou province and the picturesque West Lake back in the 12th century, and he called it a paradise on earth. It's a pity the intrepid explorer didn't bring home this soup recipe . . . he would have called it paradise in a soup pot.

Makes 4 to 6 servings

Marinade

3 TABLESPOONS WATER

2 TABLESPOONS Chinese RICE WINE OR
DRY SHERRY

1 TABLESPOON CORNSTARCH

✦ ✦ ✦

8 OUNCES LEAN GROUND BEEF

1 QUART BEEF STOCK

1 QUART COLD WATER

3 TABLESPOONS SOY SAUCE

1 TEASPOON CHILE OIL

WHITE PEPPER

1 SMALL LEEK, JULIENNED

¾ CUP FROZEN PEAS, THAWED

½ CARROT, DICED

2 TABLESPOONS CHOPPED CILANTRO

1 SHEET JAPANESE SEAWEED (NORI),
TORN INTO SMALL PIECES

¼ CUP CORNSTARCH DISSOLVED
IN ¼ CUP WATER

2 EGGS, LIGHTLY BEATEN

1 TEASPOON SESAME OIL

Combine the marinade ingredients in a bowl. Separate the ground beef into small bits. In a pot of boiling water, blanch the beef, stirring to separate, for 1 minute; drain. Add the beef to the marinade and stir to coat. Let stand for 10 minutes.

In a large pot, bring the stock and water to a boil over medium-high heat. Add the soy sauce and chile oil. If desired, add a dash of white pepper to give it a little kick. Add the beef, leek, peas, carrot, and cilantro. Reduce the heat to low and simmer, uncovered, for 5 minutes. Add the seaweed. Add the cornstarch mixture and cook, stirring, until the soup boils and thickens slightly.

Remove the soup from the heat and slowly drizzle in the eggs, stirring in one direction until the eggs form short threads. Stir in the sesame oil and serve immediately.

BEIJING HOT AND SOUR SOUP

Nothing perks up the appetite quite like the combination of spicy and sour tastes. I make it a practice to cook extra portions of entrées when I serve hot and sour soup as a starter. My guests always have a healthy appetite after a bowl of this.

Makes 6 to 8 servings

1 TABLESPOON DRIED SHRIMP

2 DRIED WOOD EAR MUSHROOMS

1½ QUARTS CHICKEN STOCK

7 OUNCES SOFT TOFU, DRAINED AND
  DICED

4 OUNCES BAMBOO SHOOTS, JULIENNED

4 OUNCES BONELESS LEAN PORK,
  THINLY SLICED

2 TABLESPOONS SHREDDED SICHUAN
  PRESERVED VEGETABLE

⅓ CUP RICE VINEGAR

¼ CUP LIGHT SOY SAUCE

1 TABLESPOON DARK SOY SAUCE

2 TEASPOONS CHILE GARLIC SAUCE

1 TEASPOON SESAME OIL

¾ TEASPOON WHITE PEPPER

½ TEASPOON SUGAR

¼ CUP CORNSTARCH DISSOLVED IN
  ¼ CUP WATER

1 EGG, LIGHTLY BEATEN

CHOPPED CILANTRO

SLIVERED GREEN ONION

Soak the shrimp in warm water to cover for 20 minutes; drain. Coarsely chop the shrimp. Soak the wood ear mushrooms in warm water to cover until softened, about 15 minutes, then shred them; reserve the mushroom soaking liquid.

In a large pot, bring the stock and reserved mushroom soaking liquid to a boil over medium-high heat. Add the mushrooms, shrimp, tofu, bamboo shoots, pork, and preserved vegetable. Cook, stirring occasionally, for 3 minutes. Add the vinegar, light and dark soy sauces, chile garlic sauce, sesame oil, pepper, and sugar. Reduce the heat to low and simmer for 3 more minutes. Add the cornstarch mixture and cook, stirring, until the soup boils and thickens slightly.

Remove the soup from the heat and slowly drizzle in the egg, stirring in one direction until the egg forms short threads. Garnish with cilantro and green onion and serve immediately.

BOK CHOY SOUP WITH CRAB

*Bok choy is a popular leafy vegetable that you will find in many
Chinese soups. Its mild, sweet taste and crunchy texture go well with
any meat, seafood, or other ingredients. Here it gets on swimmingly
with crabmeat, ginger, and shallots.*

Makes 4 servings

2 TEASPOONS COOKING OIL

2 SLICES GINGER, LIGHTLY CRUSHED

1 WALNUT-SIZED SHALLOT, FINELY
   CHOPPED

4 OUNCES COOKED CRABMEAT, FLAKED

1 QUART CHICKEN STOCK

1 CUP COLD WATER

2 TEASPOONS SOY SAUCE

8 OUNCES BOK CHOY, THINLY SLICED

1 CARROT, SLICED

1/2 TEASPOON SESAME OIL

1/4 TEASPOON WHITE PEPPER

Place a pot over high heat until hot. Add the oil, swirling to coat the sides.
Add the ginger and shallot and cook, stirring, until fragrant, about 10
seconds. Add the crabmeat and stir-fry for 1 minute.

Add the stock, water, and soy sauce; bring to a boil. Add the bok choy and
carrot. Reduce the heat to low and simmer until the vegetables are tender,
about 5 minutes. Stir in the sesame oil and pepper.

Salads are relatively new to Chinese cooking. This is not to say, however, that the Chinese don't like vegetables. In fact, we love them! In a typical Chinese dish, you are bound to find more vegetables than meat or poultry.

All good cuisines evolve and adopt new techniques and ingredients from other cultures. In recent years, creative Chinese chefs have gone abroad to receive training in Western cuisines, and many of them are in turn giving Western salads a Chinese touch. This chapter includes many such recipes.

With all their help and mine, there is absolutely no excuse not to eat your vegetables and enjoy them!

SALADS

SALADS

CHINATOWN CHICKEN SALAD

You will find this dish on the menus of Chinese restaurants from Beijing to Buenos Aires, but it is also very easy to make at home. And what a great way to use up that extra cooked chicken.

Makes 4 servings

8 OUNCES SHREDDED ICEBERG LETTUCE

5 OUNCES SHREDDED COOKED CHICKEN

1 CARROT, CUT INTO MATCHSTICK
  PIECES

2 OUNCES FRESH MUNG BEAN SPROUTS

¼ CUP CILANTRO LEAVES

2 TABLESPOONS SHREDDED PICKLED
  GINGER

• • •

½ CUP SLICED ALMONDS

1 TEASPOON SESAME SEEDS

Dressing

3 TABLESPOONS COOKING OIL

1 TEASPOON FINELY CHOPPED GINGER

1 TEASPOON FINELY CHOPPED GARLIC

2 GREEN ONIONS, JULIENNED

¼ CUP RICE VINEGAR

2 TABLESPOONS SOY SAUCE

1 TABLESPOON HONEY

2 TEASPOONS SESAME OIL

1 TEASPOON CHILE OIL

½ TEASPOON BLACK PEPPER

• • •

COOKING OIL FOR DEEP-FRYING

5 THICK WONTON WRAPPERS, CUT INTO
  ¼-INCH STRIPS

In a large salad bowl, combine the lettuce, chicken, carrot, bean sprouts, cilantro, and pickled ginger; refrigerate.

Preheat the oven to 350°. Spread the almonds in a shallow baking pan. Toast, shaking the pan occasionally, until golden brown, 5 to 10 minutes. Place the sesame seeds in a small frying pan over medium heat; cook, shaking the pan frequently, until seeds are lightly browned, 3 to 4 minutes. Immediately remove from the pan and let cool.

To make the dressing, place a small pan over medium-high heat until hot. Add the oil, swirling to coat the sides. Add the ginger, garlic, and green onions; cook, stirring, for 1 minute. Add the vinegar, soy sauce, honey, sesame oil, chile oil, and pepper. Cook, stirring, until the mixture comes to a boil. Remove the pan from the heat.

In a wok, heat the oil to 375°. Deep-fry the wonton strips, half at a time, until golden brown, about 5 minutes. Remove and drain on paper towels.

Just before serving, drizzle the dressing over the salad and toss to coat. Sprinkle the toasted almonds and sesame seeds over the salad. Top with the wonton strips and serve.

CHINESE CAESAR SALAD

Julius Caesar didn't conquer China, but Caesar salad certainly has. The crunch of rice cakes and freshly toasted walnuts provides excellent contrast to the bed of crisp romaine lettuce—a triumph worthy of a Caesar.

Makes 4 to 6 servings

Creamy Sesame Tofu Dressing

2 TABLESPOONS BLANCHED ALMONDS

2 TO 3 CLOVES GARLIC

8 OUNCES SOFT TOFU, DRAINED

1 TO 2 TEASPOONS (OR MORE) MASHED
    CANNED ANCHOVIES (OPTIONAL)

3 TABLESPOONS DIJON MUSTARD

¼ CUP WATER (OPTIONAL)

3 TABLESPOONS FRESHLY SQUEEZED
    LEMON JUICE

2 TABLESPOONS SOY SAUCE

2 TEASPOONS SESAME OIL

1 TEASPOON FISH SAUCE

⅓ CUP WALNUTS

COOKING OIL FOR DEEP-FRYING

½ OUNCE STORE-BOUGHT DRIED RICE
    CRUSTS (SEE PAGE 37)

10 OUNCES ROMAINE LETTUCE, WASHED
    AND TORN INTO BITE-SIZE PIECES

1 OUNCE DRIED ANCHOVIES

Place the almonds and garlic in a blender; process until well ground. Add the remaining dressing ingredients; process until smooth. If dressing is too thick, add enough water to make desired consistency. (If a stronger anchovy flavor is desired, increase amount of anchovies.) Cover and refrigerate until chilled.

Preheat the oven to 350°. Spread the walnuts in a shallow baking pan. Toast, shaking the pan occasionally, until golden brown, 5 to 10 minutes.

In a wok, heat the oil for deep-frying to 375°. Deep-fry the rice crusts, half at a time, until puffed, about 5 seconds. Lift out with a slotted spoon and drain well on paper towels. Break gently into small pieces.

Place the lettuce in a salad bowl. Drizzle the dressing over the salad; toss to coat. Sprinkle the walnuts, rice crusts, and dried anchovies over the salad and serve.

Wall to Wall Nuts

Walnuts are the oldest tree food harvested by man, dating back to 7000 BC. In China, walnuts have been grown for more than 1,500 years. The cooks in the western province of Sichuan toast walnuts, grind them to make sweets, and chop them to coat fried food. They even make walnut tea. My favorite way to enjoy walnuts is with a honey glaze— a fabulous snack.

PICKLED VEGETABLES

Whoever says vegetables are boring has not tasted my pickled cabbage. The fresh red and green jalapeño chiles make this anything but bland, and it's bound to perk up your appetite for the main course.

Makes 10 servings

2 RED BELL PEPPERS, SEEDED

½ CABBAGE

½ JICAMA, OR 8 OUNCES CANNED
    WHOLE WATER CHESTNUTS,
    CUT IN HALF

1 GREEN JALAPEÑO CHILE

1 RED JALAPEÑO CHILE

1 CARROT, SLICED

10 SLICES GINGER

8 WALNUT-SIZED SHALLOTS, THINLY
    SLICED

2 TEASPOONS SALT

Pickling Solution

1 TEASPOON SICHUAN PEPPERCORNS

2 CUPS RICE VINEGAR

1¼ CUPS SUGAR

1¼ TEASPOONS SALT

½ TEASPOON DRIED RED PEPPER FLAKES

In a Pickle

Before the invention of refrigeration, keeping produce fresh was a problem. Chinese preserved vegetables by pickling them in urns and jars. The Korean version is the spicy kimchee. A tip on pickling: for best results, use salt without additives. Regular table salt is iodized and contains other additives.

Cut the bell peppers, cabbage, and jicama into 1- to 1½-inch chunks. Cut the green and red jalapeños in half and discard the seeds.

Place the bell peppers, cabbage, jicama, jalapeños, carrot, ginger, and shallots in a large bowl; rub salt into them with your hands. Cover the vegetables with a plate, weight it with a heavy can, and let stand at room temperature for 1 hour.

Place the peppercorns in a frying pan over medium heat. Cook, shaking the pan frequently, until the peppercorns darken slightly and smell toasted, 3 to 4 minutes. Add the vinegar, sugar, salt, and pepper flakes to the pan. Cook, stirring, over medium-high heat until the sugar dissolves, 2 to 3 minutes. Let stand until cool.

Pour the vegetable mixture into a colander and rinse well to remove the salty liquid. Place the vegetables in a self-sealing plastic bag or in a nonreactive bowl. Pour the pickling solution over the vegetables. Seal the bag or cover the bowl with plastic wrap. Refrigerate for at least 2 days or up to 1 week.

SQUID SALAD WITH LIME DRESSING

The crunchy texture of squid makes it a great salad ingredient. Remember that snow peas cook in a hurry, so if you like their fresh-tasting crunch (and who doesn't?), you'd better rescue them from the boiling water after no more than a minute or two.

Makes 4 servings

1 POUND SMALL SQUID, CLEANED

2 OUNCES SNOW PEAS, ENDS AND
  STRINGS REMOVED

Lime Dressing

2 TABLESPOONS RICE VINEGAR

2 TABLESPOONS FRESHLY SQUEEZED
  LIME JUICE

2 TABLESPOONS SESAME OIL

2 TABLESPOONS SUGAR

1 TABLESPOON SOY SAUCE

1 TEASPOON FINELY CHOPPED GARLIC

$\frac{1}{2}$ TEASPOON SALT

$\frac{1}{4}$ TEASPOON DRIED RED PEPPER FLAKES

• • •

1 CARROT, CUT INTO MATCHSTICK
  PIECES

$\frac{1}{2}$ CUCUMBER, PEELED, SEEDED, AND
  CUT INTO MATCHSTICK PIECES

4 OUNCES FRESH MUNG BEAN SPROUTS

$\frac{1}{4}$ CUP CILANTRO LEAVES, COARSELY
  CHOPPED

Cut the squid bodies into $\frac{1}{4}$-inch rings. Leave the tentacles whole. Cut the snow peas in half diagonally.

In a bowl, combine the dressing ingredients; whisk until smooth.

In a pot of boiling water, cook the squid, including the tentacles, for 1 minute. Drain, rinse with cold running water, and drain again. Remove the squid to a bowl. Add 2 tablespoons of the dressing and toss to coat. Let stand for 30 minutes.

In a pot of boiling water, cook the snow peas and carrot until tender-crisp, about 1 minute. Drain, rinse with cold running water, and drain again.

Place the squid in a salad bowl. Add the snow peas, carrot, cucumber, bean sprouts, and cilantro; mix well. Add the remaining dressing and toss to coat.

Dressing for Success

Here's a simple tip that will save you time in the kitchen. You know that great salad dressing you made for last night's meal? Well, if you had had the foresight to make extra, tonight you could have the same great dressing without any fuss. When properly refrigerated, salad dressing can last a few days, so don't be shy about making extra. You are saving yourself time that could be better used for important things . . . like planning your next salad adventure!

DUCK SALAD WITH SEASONAL FRUIT

Savory duck meat provides an interesting taste contrast to the sweetness of fresh fruits. Toss in some greens and walnuts and you and your guests are in for a super salad treat. For this recipe you may use any fresh fruit in season, but my personal favorites are persimmons and Asian pears.

Makes 2 main dish servings; 4 to 6 side dish servings

10 OUNCES MIXED SALAD GREENS

1 STALK CELERY, THINLY SLICED
   DIAGONALLY

1 CRISP PERSIMMON OR ASIAN PEAR,
   CUT INTO THIN WEDGES

• • •

½ CUP WALNUTS

½ CHINESE ROAST DUCK OR 2 CHINESE
   ROAST DUCK BREASTS

Dressing

¼ CUP APRICOT PRESERVES

2 TABLESPOONS SEASONED RICE
   VINEGAR

2 TABLESPOONS COOKING OIL

1 TEASPOON SESAME OIL

1 TEASPOON PREPARED CHINESE
   MUSTARD

1 TEASPOON GRATED GINGER

In a large salad bowl, combine the salad greens, celery, and persimmon; toss well. Cover and refrigerate. Whisk the dressing ingredients together in a bowl.

Preheat the oven to 350°. Spread the walnuts in a shallow baking pan. Toast, shaking the pan occasionally, until golden brown, 5 to 10 minutes.

Cut the duck breast from the carcass in one piece, with the skin attached. Cut it crosswise into ¼-inch-thick slices. Remove the remaining meat from the carcass and shred it.

Place the shredded meat in the salad; toss to combine. Add half the dressing; toss to coat. Arrange the sliced breast over the salad. Sprinkle the toasted walnuts over all. Serve with the remaining dressing passed alongside.

CLAM SALAD WITH RICE VINEGAR DRESSING

This salad is served cold and uses fresh clams. If they are not available, good-quality canned clams or frozen clams, rinsed and patted dry, work very well.

Makes 4 servings

Dressing

1 TEASPOON SESAME SEEDS
3 TABLESPOONS RICE VINEGAR
1 TABLESPOON SOY SAUCE
1/2 TEASPOON SUGAR
1/8 TEASPOON WHITE PEPPER

1 POUND SMALL HARD-SHELL CLAMS, WELL SCRUBBED AND COOKED
4 GREEN ONIONS, THINLY SLICED
2 TABLESPOONS CHOPPED CILANTRO
LETTUCE LEAVES
THINLY SLICED CUCUMBER

Place sesame seeds in a small frying pan over medium heat; cook, shaking the pan frequently, until seeds are lightly browned, 3 to 4 minutes. Immediately remove from pan to cool. In a salad bowl, whisk together the sesame seeds with the remaining dressing ingredients.

Remove the cooked clams from their shells. Add the clams, green onions, and cilantro to the dressing; toss well.

Arrange the lettuce leaves on a serving plate. Spoon the clam salad into the middle and garnish with cucumber slices.

RED PEPPER AND CUCUMBER SALAD

The saying "cool as a cucumber" won't apply to this fiery dish after you add the chiles. Maybe we should have a new saying, "hot as a cucumber!"

Makes 4 servings

1/4 CUP RICE VINEGAR
2 TABLESPOONS SESAME OIL
6 CLOVES GARLIC, THINLY SLICED
2 TEASPOONS SALT
2 TEASPOONS SUGAR

1 CUCUMBER, CUT IN HALF AND THINLY SLICED
1 RED BELL PEPPER, SEEDED AND THINLY SLICED
1 GREEN ONION, CHOPPED
1/2 TEASPOON DRIED RED PEPPER FLAKES

In a bowl, combine the vinegar, sesame oil, garlic, salt, and sugar. Add the cucumber, bell pepper, green onion, and pepper flakes; toss to coat. Let stand for 5 minutes. Drain well before serving.

One Size Fits All

The English cucumber is raised in a hothouse, and it can reach more than a foot in length. It has a bright green skin and is practically seedless. Its Japanese counterpart is similar but measures only about an inch in diameter and 8 inches in length.

Spicy Spinach Salad

My earliest memory of spinach was in my soup, but since then I have discovered that wilted spinach can make a wonderful salad, especially when you serve it with a dressing spiked with cider vinegar and chile garlic sauce.

Makes 4 servings

8 OUNCES BABY SPINACH

½ RED BELL PEPPER, SEEDED AND
    THINLY SLICED

½ SMALL RED ONION, THINLY SLICED

2 TABLESPOONS COARSELY CHOPPED
    MINT

2 TABLESPOONS COARSELY CHOPPED
    CILANTRO

Dressing

2 TABLESPOONS COOKING OIL

3 OUNCES CHINESE SAUSAGES *(LOP
    CHEONG)*, THINLY SLICED DIAGONALLY

2 TEASPOONS FINELY CHOPPED GARLIC

1 TEASPOON FINELY CHOPPED GINGER

¼ CUP CIDER VINEGAR

2 TABLESPOONS SOY SAUCE

1 TABLESPOON SUGAR

1 TABLESPOON CHILE GARLIC SAUCE

Wash the spinach and remove the tough stems. If the spinach leaves are large, tear into smaller pieces. Place the spinach in a salad bowl. Add the bell pepper, onion, mint, and cilantro; toss to mix.

Place a pan over high heat until hot. Add the oil, swirling to coat the sides. Add the sausages; stir-fry for 30 seconds. Add the garlic and ginger; cook, stirring, until fragrant, about 10 seconds. Add the vinegar, soy sauce, sugar, and chile garlic sauce; cook, stirring, until the sugar dissolves.

Pour the hot dressing over the salad and toss to coat. Allow the spinach to wilt before serving.

CHILLED NOODLES WITH FISH CAKES

This Chinese-style pasta salad is light, refreshing, and easy to make.
Follow the simple steps and it's a real piece of cake; fish cake, that is.

Makes 6 to 8 servings

2 TABLESPOONS WHITE SESAME SEEDS

2 TABLESPOONS BLACK SESAME SEEDS

Dressing

¼ CUP CHICKEN STOCK

¼ CUP RICE VINEGAR

1½ TABLESPOONS SOY SAUCE

1 TABLESPOON SUGAR

1 TABLESPOON CHINESE RICE WINE OR
DRY SHERRY

1½ TEASPOONS SESAME OIL

1½ TEASPOONS CHILE OIL

＊ ＊ ＊

12 OUNCES FRESH CHINESE EGG
NOODLES

1 CUCUMBER

1 RED BELL PEPPER, SEEDED

2 GREEN ONIONS

8 OUNCES STORE-BOUGHT FISH CAKES

2 TABLESPOONS CHOPPED CILANTRO

MINT SPRIGS

Place white sesame seeds in a small frying pan over medium heat; cook, shaking pan frequently, until seeds are lightly browned, 3 to 4 minutes. Immediately remove from pan to cool. Place black sesame seeds in a small frying pan over medium heat; cook, shaking pan frequently, until seeds smell toasted, 3 to 4 minutes. Immediately remove from pan to cool.

Combine the dressing ingredients in a bowl.

Bring a pot of water to a boil. Add the noodles and cook according to the package directions. Drain, rinse with cold running water, and drain again. Place the noodles in a large bowl. Pour half of the dressing over the noodles and toss to coat. Refrigerate until chilled, about 30 minutes.

Cut the cucumber and bell pepper into matchstick pieces. Cut the green onions into 1½-inch slivers. Cut the fish cakes into 1½-inch slices.

Just before serving, top the noodles with the vegetables, fish cakes, cilantro, and remaining dressing. Sprinkle with the sesame seeds and garnish with the mint.

CHILLED NOODLES WITH SHREDDED CHICKEN

Here's a perfect dish for a hot summer night. Make it ahead of time, and simply toss with the dressing at the last minute. Chilled noodles are very popular in Sichuan province, which has more than its share of hot summer nights.

Makes 4 servings

2 TABLESPOONS SICHUAN PEPPERCORNS

2 TABLESPOONS SESAME SEEDS

12 OUNCES FRESH CHINESE EGG
    NOODLES

2 TEASPOONS SESAME OIL

1 CARROT, JULIENNED

½ CUCUMBER, JULIENNED

2½ OUNCES FRESH MUNG BEAN
    SPROUTS

9 OUNCES SHREDDED COOKED CHICKEN

Fresh Herb Dressing

⅓ CUP CHICKEN STOCK

3 TABLESPOONS SESAME SEED PASTE OR
    CHUNKY PEANUT BUTTER

2 TABLESPOONS SEASONED RICE
    VINEGAR

1 TABLESPOON SOY SAUCE

2 TEASPOONS CHILE GARLIC SAUCE

2 TEASPOONS SESAME OIL

2 TABLESPOONS CHOPPED BASIL

2 TEASPOONS CHOPPED CILANTRO

Sassy Sesame

In Chinese cooking, the flavor of sesame seeds comes three ways:
(1) Dark amber-colored sesame oil pressed from toasted white sesame seeds; use a few drops in marinades, dressings, and stir-fries.
(2) Sesame paste, a thick paste with a roasted nutty taste and aroma.
(3) Toasted sesame seeds (in particular the white seeds); they're very aromatic and make a great garnish, too.

Place the peppercorns in a small frying pan over medium heat. Cook, shaking pan frequently, until the peppercorns darken slightly and smell toasted, 3 to 4 minutes. Process in a spice grinder or blender until coarsely ground. Place the sesame seeds in a small frying pan over medium heat; cook, shaking the pan frequently, until seeds are lightly browned, 3 to 4 minutes. Remove from the pan immediately to cool.

Bring a pot of water to a boil. Add the noodles and cook according to the package directions. Drain, rinse with cold running water, and drain again. In a bowl, toss the noodles with the sesame oil.

Add the carrot, cucumber, and bean sprouts; toss to mix. Place on a serving platter and arrange the chicken on top. Cover and chill.

In a bowl, whisk the stock and sesame seed paste until blended. Add the rice vinegar, soy sauce, chile garlic sauce, sesame oil, basil, and cilantro; mix well.

Pour the dressing over the noodles and toss before serving. Garnish with the ground peppercorns and sesame seeds.

NOODLES WITH SMOKED PRESSED TOFU

The slightly chewy texture of bean thread noodles provides a contrast to the pressed tofu, crunchy carrot, and roasted peanuts. And the sharp-tasting dressing adds an extra kick. If you can't find smoked pressed tofu, use regular pressed tofu.

Makes 4 servings

8 OUNCES DRIED BEAN THREAD
   NOODLES

Dressing

$\frac{1}{2}$ CUP FRESHLY SQUEEZED LEMON
   JUICE

$\frac{1}{3}$ CUP COOKING OIL

$\frac{1}{4}$ CUP SUGAR

3 TABLESPOONS FINELY CHOPPED
   GINGER

2 TABLESPOONS SOY SAUCE

4 TEASPOONS SESAME OIL

2 TEASPOONS FINELY CHOPPED GARLIC

1 TEASPOON CHILE SAUCE

$\frac{1}{2}$ TEASPOON WHITE PEPPER

$4\frac{1}{2}$ OUNCES SEASONED PRESSED TOFU,
   CUT INTO MATCHSTICK PIECES

$\frac{1}{2}$ RED ONION, THINLY SLICED

$\frac{1}{2}$ CUCUMBER, CUT INTO MATCHSTICK
   PIECES

1 CARROT, CUT INTO MATCHSTICK
   PIECES

$\frac{1}{2}$ CUP UNSALTED ROASTED PEANUTS

Soak the bean thread noodles in warm water to cover until softened, about 30 minutes; drain. Bring a pot of water to a boil. Add the noodles and cook for 3 to 4 minutes. Drain, rinse with cold running water, and drain again. Cut the noodles in half.

Combine the dressing ingredients in a bowl.

Place the noodles, tofu, onion, cucumber, and carrot in a bowl; toss to combine. Add the dressing and toss to coat. Sprinkle with the peanuts.

Hot Off the Press

Tofu (bean curd) is made from soybeans and water. It comes in three categories: firm, regular, and soft or silky. When tofu is being made, water is squeezed out by a press. The softer the tofu, the higher the water content it retains. Pressed tofu is seasoned first, then pressed extra-hard to give it that spongy texture.

SPICY GREEN BEAN SALAD

In my youth, my mom never had trouble getting us to eat our vegetables. All she had to do was sprinkle them with some sesame seeds. As an adult, I am not so easily bribed. However, a spicy dressing will make me clean my vegetable plate every time.

Makes 4 servings

Spicy Sesame Dressing

¼ CUP SESAME SEEDS
⅓ CUP SEASONED RICE VINEGAR
¼ CUP HOISIN SAUCE
1 TEASPOON CHILE GARLIC SAUCE

• • •

1 POUND GREEN BEANS
1 QUART WATER
1 TEASPOON COOKING OIL
¼ TEASPOON SALT
BLACK SESAME SEEDS (OPTIONAL)
CHOPPED RED JALAPEÑO CHILE

Mr. Beans

The crunchy texture of green beans makes them a wonderful ingredient for salads and stir-fry dishes. My childhood favorite was Chinese long beans, also known as yard-long beans. They are long, dark green, and thinner than regular green beans. They are also drier, denser, and crunchier.

Place the sesame seeds in a small frying pan over medium heat; cook, shaking the pan frequently, until the seeds are lightly browned, 3 to 4 minutes. Immediately remove from the pan to cool. Place the sesame seeds in a blender; process until well ground. Add the remaining dressing ingredients; process until smooth.

Remove and discard the ends and strings from the beans. Cut diagonally into 2-inch pieces.

In a pot, bring the water to a boil over high heat. Add the oil and salt. Add the beans and cook until tender-crisp, about 3 minutes. Drain, rinse with cold running water, and drain again. Refrigerate in a bowl until chilled. Just before serving, pour the dressing over the beans and toss to coat. Garnish with black sesame seeds and chopped jalapeño.

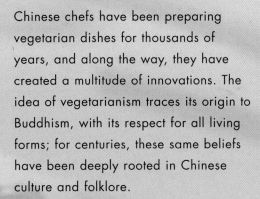

Chinese chefs have been preparing vegetarian dishes for thousands of years, and along the way, they have created a multitude of innovations. The idea of vegetarianism traces its origin to Buddhism, with its respect for all living forms; for centuries, these same beliefs have been deeply rooted in Chinese culture and folklore.

Religious beliefs notwithstanding, a Chinese chef may get by without meat, poultry, or seafood, but he cannot make do without grains and vegetables. The average Chinese dish contains more vegetables than meat or other animal protein. On special occasions such as the first day of Chinese New Year, vegetarian dishes are always served. One could easily assume that the Chinese were practicing vegetarianism long before the current trend.

Over the past decade, I've been heartened to see more and more Chinese and Asian vegetables becoming available in the West. What once was considered exotic is now commonly displayed in Chinatown produce stores and even some local markets. Meanwhile, snow peas, bean sprouts, fresh ginger, and packaged tofu are becoming commonplace in the fruit and vegetable section of local supermarkets.

Growing up in Guangzhou, we never had to be told to eat our vegetables. Follow the recipes in this chapter, and you will see why.

SICHUAN EGGPLANT

I know several Chinese restaurants in New York where people wait in line for an hour just for a taste of eggplant cooked Sichuan-style, with spicy garlic sauce. Now you have the secret recipe. Follow it and watch the line outside your kitchen grow.

Makes 4 servings

Sauce

½ CUP CHICKEN STOCK

2 TABLESPOONS SOY SAUCE

2 TABLESPOONS CHINESE BLACK
    VINEGAR OR BALSAMIC VINEGAR

1 TABLESPOON HOISIN SAUCE

2 TEASPOONS CHILE PASTE

• • •

1½ POUNDS ASIAN EGGPLANT

COOKING OIL FOR DEEP-FRYING

1 TABLESPOON FINELY CHOPPED GARLIC

2 OUNCES CHOPPED BONELESS PORK

2 GREEN ONIONS, SLICED

½ TEASPOON CORNSTARCH DISSOLVED
    IN 1 TEASPOON WATER

¼ CUP BASIL LEAVES

To Meat or Not to Meat

The traditional recipe for Sichuan Eggplant calls for a small amount of pork, more as a flavoring than a main ingredient. Strict vegetarians can always leave out the pork and let the spicy garlic sauce carry the day.

Combine the sauce ingredients in a bowl. Roll-cut the eggplant.

In a wok, heat the oil for deep-frying to 375°. Deep-fry the eggplant until golden brown, about 2 minutes. Remove and drain on paper towels.

Remove all but 2 tablespoons of oil from the wok. Place over high heat until hot. Add the garlic and cook, stirring, until fragrant, about 10 seconds. Add the pork; cook, stirring, until the pork is browned and crumbly, about 1½ minutes. Add the eggplant, green onions, and sauce; bring to a boil. Reduce the heat to medium; cover and cook until the eggplant is tender, 5 to 6 minutes. Add the cornstarch mixture and cook, stirring, until the sauce boils and thickens. Stir in the basil.

Eggplant with Jade Sauce

The flavor of fresh mint is becoming very popular in contemporary Chinese cooking. These aromatic leaves are as pleasing to the eye as they are to your nose and palate.

Makes 4 servings

1½ POUNDS ASIAN EGGPLANT

1½ QUARTS WATER

2 TEASPOONS SALT

COOKING OIL FOR DEEP-FRYING

3 CLOVES GARLIC, SLICED

¼ CUP MINT LEAVES

Sauce

½ CUP CHICKEN STOCK

2 TABLESPOONS LIGHT SOY SAUCE

1 TABLESPOON DARK SOY SAUCE

2 TEASPOONS SESAME OIL

1½ TEASPOONS SUGAR

1½ TEASPOONS MUSTARD POWDER

◆ ◆ ◆

1½ TEASPOONS CORNSTARCH DISSOLVED IN 1 TABLESPOON WATER

Cut the eggplant into 2- by 1½-inch strips. Place the eggplant in a bowl. Add the water and salt; mix well. Let stand for 15 minutes; drain. Squeeze gently to remove the excess liquid.

In a wok, heat the oil for deep-frying to 375°. Deep-fry the garlic until golden brown, about 30 seconds. Remove and drain on paper towels. Deep-fry the mint leaves until glossy, about 30 seconds. Remove and drain on paper towels.

Bring a pot of water to a boil. Add the eggplant and return to a boil. Reduce the heat to low. Cover and simmer until tender but still firm, about 15 minutes; drain.

Place the fried garlic in a pan. Add the sauce ingredients and bring to a boil over medium-high heat. Add the cornstarch mixture and cook, stirring, until the sauce boils and thickens.

To serve, place the eggplant on a serving platter. Pour the sauce over all and garnish with the mint leaves.

CHINESE BROCCOLI WITH OYSTER SAUCE

If you ever go into a Chinese noodle shop, you will probably find this dish on every other table. This is a very popular way of serving the leafy Chinese broccoli (gai lan) as a side dish. Cook this at home, and in minutes your kitchen will seem like an authentic Chinese restaurant.

Makes 4 servings

Sauce

2 TABLESPOONS OYSTER SAUCE

1 TEASPOON CHINESE RICE WINE OR
   DRY SHERRY

1 TEASPOON SESAME OIL

½ TEASPOON CHILE GARLIC SAUCE

2 SLICES GINGER, JULIENNED

12 OUNCES CHINESE BROCCOLI OR
   REGULAR BROCCOLI

2 TABLESPOONS COOKING OIL

1 TEASPOON SALT

Combine the sauce ingredients in a bowl.

Trim the Chinese broccoli and cut the stalks into thirds. If using regular broccoli, peel off the tough skin on the stems. Cut the tops into florets and cut the stems diagonally into thin slices.

Bring a pot of water to a boil. Add the oil, salt, and broccoli; cook until the broccoli is tender-crisp, about 4 minutes. Drain well and place on a serving platter. Drizzle the sauce over the broccoli.

Flavor of an Oyster

Thick, dark brown oyster sauce is made from an extract of oysters combined with sugar, salt, caramel, and starch. Look for it in bottles or cans; once it's opened, you should store it in the refrigerator. If you're a vegetarian, look for vegetarian oyster sauce, which is made with dried mushrooms.

SWEET AND TANGY ASPARAGUS

While asparagus has been the vegetable of kings in Europe for centuries, it is a relative newcomer to Chinese cooking. There is nothing like making up for lost time. We, too, can aspire to asparagus, especially when it is served in this sweet and tangy sauce. This dish can be served chilled or at room temperature.

Makes 4 servings

1 TABLESPOON SESAME SEEDS

1 TEASPOON COOKING OIL

½ TEASPOON SALT

1 POUND ASPARAGUS, TRIMMED AND
   CUT DIAGONALLY INTO 1½-INCH
   SLICES

Sauce

¼ CUP SEASONED RICE VINEGAR

2 TABLESPOONS SOY SAUCE

1 TABLESPOON SESAME OIL

2 TEASPOONS HONEY

1 TEASPOON CHILE GARLIC SAUCE

1 TEASPOON FINELY CHOPPED GARLIC

1 TEASPOON FINELY CHOPPED GINGER

• • •

1 TEASPOON CORNSTARCH DISSOLVED IN
   2 TEASPOONS WATER

Place the sesame seeds in a small frying pan over medium heat; cook, shaking the pan frequently, until the seeds are lightly browned, 3 to 4 minutes. Immediately remove from the pan to cool.

Bring a pot of water to a boil. Add the oil and salt, followed by the asparagus; cook until the asparagus is tender-crisp, 1 to 2 minutes. Drain, rinse with cold running water, and drain again. Pat dry with paper towels, then place in a bowl.

Combine the sauce ingredients in a pan. Bring to a boil over medium-high heat. Add the cornstarch mixture and cook, stirring, until the sauce boils and thickens.

Pour the sauce over the asparagus and toss to coat. Let stand for 3 minutes.

Place the asparagus on a serving platter. Sprinkle the sesame seeds over the asparagus and serve.

Cooling Off

A sure way to keep from overcooking asparagus (and keep it from losing its bright green color) is to blanch it in boiling water, then immediately immerse the spears in cold running water. Drain them, then use in your favorite recipes.

TWICE-COOKED GREEN BEANS WITH MEAT SAUCE

Twice-cooking is a technique that is ideal for green beans. The hot oil gets rid of the water in the beans and brings out their natural sweetness. When the beans are then stir-fried with seasonings, they absorb all the wonderful flavors of the other ingredients.

Makes 4 servings

2 TABLESPOONS DRIED SHRIMP

Sauce

¼ CUP CHICKEN STOCK

1 TABLESPOON DARK SOY SAUCE

1 TABLESPOON LIGHT SOY SAUCE

½ TEASPOON SESAME OIL

1 POUND GREEN BEANS

COOKING OIL FOR DEEP-FRYING

2 TEASPOONS FINELY CHOPPED GARLIC

2 TABLESPOONS CHOPPED SICHUAN
  PRESERVED VEGETABLE

1 TEASPOON DRIED RED PEPPER FLAKES

4 OUNCES GROUND LEAN PORK

1 TEASPOON CORNSTARCH DISSOLVED IN
  1 TABLESPOON WATER

Soak the shrimp in warm water to cover for 20 minutes; drain. Coarsely chop the shrimp. Combine the sauce ingredients in a bowl. Remove and discard the ends and strings from the beans. Cut into 2-inch pieces.

In a wok, heat the oil for deep-frying to 360°. Add the beans, half at a time, and cook until the beans become wrinkled, about 2 minutes. Remove and drain on paper towels.

Remove all but 1 tablespoon oil from the wok. Place over high heat until hot. Add the garlic, shrimp, preserved vegetable, and pepper flakes; cook, stirring, until fragrant, about 30 seconds. Add the pork and cook, stirring, until browned and crumbly, about 1½ minutes. Add the beans and sauce; bring to a boil. Add the cornstarch mixture and cook, stirring, until the sauce boils and thickens.

CABBAGE WITH CREAMY SAUCE AND CHAR SIU

Milk and cream are not prominently featured in Chinese cooking, but things are changing. Adaptability is the key to the longevity of any cuisine. If you cannot find char siu *(Chinese barbecued pork), use Chinese ham or regular ham. In cooking as in life, be flexible!*

Makes 4 servings

Sauce

¾ CUP CHICKEN STOCK

⅓ CUP EVAPORATED MILK

¼ CUP UNSWEETENED COCONUT MILK

2 TABLESPOONS CHINESE RICE WINE OR
   DRY SHERRY

1 TABLESPOON CORNSTARCH

2 TEASPOONS SUGAR

¾ TEASPOON SALT

¼ TEASPOON WHITE PEPPER

· · ·

2 TABLESPOONS COOKING OIL

1½ POUNDS NAPA CABBAGE, CUT INTO
   BITE-SIZE PIECES

2 OUNCES CHINESE BARBECUED PORK
   (*CHAR SIU*) OR CHINESE HAM,
   JULIENNED OR SLICED

CHOPPED GREEN ONIONS

Combine the sauce ingredients in a bowl.

Place a wok or wide frying pan over medium-high heat until hot. Add the oil, swirling to coat the sides. Add the cabbage and stir-fry until tender-crisp, 6 to 8 minutes. Place the cabbage on a serving platter.

Pour the sauce into the wok and cook, stirring, until the sauce boils and thickens. Spoon the sauce over the cabbage and top with the barbecued pork. Sprinkle the green onions over the cabbage and serve.

Don't Dilly, Deli

A good Chinese grocery or deli is probably the best friend any busy home cook can have. Barbecued roast pork, spareribs, roast duck, soy sauce chicken, crispy roast pork, and even a whole roast pig are there for the asking. Some delis (especially those connected to a regular restaurant) also sell quite a few popular cooked dishes to take out. Whether it's a case of being tired of leftovers or hosting last-minute guests, your trusty Chinese deli has your dinner solution.

ZUCCHINI WITH BEAN THREAD NOODLES AND DRIED SHRIMP

The Chinese name for bean thread noodles is fun see. *When cooked, they are soft and slippery, silvery and shiny (fun to see?), and they make quite a texture contrast to the stir-fried zucchini and crusty shrimp.*

Makes 4 servings

6 OUNCES DRIED BEAN THREAD
   NOODLES

2 TABLESPOONS DRIED SHRIMP

Sauce

1½ CUPS CHICKEN STOCK

2 TABLESPOONS OYSTER SAUCE

¼ TEASPOON WHITE PEPPER

2 TABLESPOONS COOKING OIL

1 TEASPOON FINELY CHOPPED GARLIC

2 ZUCCHINI, JULIENNED

4 OUNCES BABY CORN, CUT IN HALF
   LENGTHWISE

¼ CUP JULIENNED SICHUAN PRESERVED
   VEGETABLE

Using Your Noodles

Dried bean thread noodles are made from mung bean starch. They are almost transparent, look like stiff nylon fishing line, and come in different lengths and thicknesses. Soften them by soaking them in warm water for about 15 minutes before using in soups and stir-fry dishes.

Soak the bean thread noodles in warm water to cover until softened, about 15 minutes; drain. Cut the noodles into 4-inch lengths. Soak the shrimp in warm water to cover until softened, about 20 minutes; drain. Chop the shrimp. Combine the sauce ingredients in a bowl.

Place a wok or wide frying pan over high heat until hot. Add the oil, swirling to coat the sides. Add the shrimp and garlic; cook, stirring, until fragrant, about 30 seconds. Add the zucchini, corn, and preserved vegetable; stir-fry until the zucchini are tender-crisp, about 2 minutes. Add the noodles and sauce; cook until heated through, 1 to 2 minutes.

TEMPLE VEGETARIAN FEAST

Vegetarian dishes have a long tradition in the Buddhist religion. When I visited the Shaolin Temple in China, the monks were generous in sharing their recipes as well as their philosophy of a healthy life. Good physical health and mental tranquility: isn't that the definition of happiness?

Makes 4 servings

1 OUNCE SNOW PEAS, ENDS AND
   STRINGS REMOVED

½ RED BELL PEPPER, SEEDED

Seasonings

⅓ CUP CHICKEN STOCK

2 TABLESPOONS SOY SAUCE

1 TABLESPOON VEGETARIAN OYSTER
   SAUCE

¼ TEASPOON SALT

2 TABLESPOONS COOKING OIL

8 OUNCES LOTUS ROOT, PEELED AND
   SLICED

3 OUNCES WHITE BUTTON MUSHROOMS,
   SLICED

2 OUNCES BABY CORN, CUT IN HALF
   DIAGONALLY

½ TEASPOON CORNSTARCH DISSOLVED
   IN 1 TSP WATER

Cut the snow peas in half diagonally. Cut the bell pepper into 1-inch squares. Combine the seasoning ingredients in a bowl.

Place a wok or wide frying pan over high heat until hot. Add the oil, swirling to coat the sides. Add the lotus root, mushrooms, corn, snow peas, and bell pepper; stir-fry for 1½ minutes. Add the seasonings and bring to a boil. Add the cornstarch mixture and cook, stirring, until the sauce boils and thickens.

The Lotus Position

Lotus roots look like a long chain of thick off-white hard sausages. When you slice across the root, you will find many air holes (as in a piece of Swiss cheese), which run the length of the root. Lotus root is crunchy and has a slightly sweet flavor, making it an ideal ingredient in a great number of dishes.

VEGETABLE PILLOWS

Some pillows are fluffy cushions for your weary head, but these steamed cabbage bundles are a tasty treat for your stomach. They may be shaped like pillows, but they definitely will not put your taste buds to sleep.

Makes 4 servings

12 DRIED BLACK (SHIITAKE)
   MUSHROOMS
2 OUNCES DRIED BEAN THREAD
   NOODLES

Seasonings

2 TABLESPOONS VEGETARIAN OYSTER
   SAUCE
2 TEASPOONS CORNSTARCH
1 TEASPOON SESAME OIL
1/8 TEASPOON WHITE PEPPER

1 TABLESPOON COOKING OIL
1 ONION, SLICED
1 CARROT, JULIENNED
2 STALKS CELERY, JULIENNED
8 LARGE CABBAGE LEAVES

Soak the mushrooms in warm water to cover until softened, about 15 minutes; drain. Discard the stems and thinly slice the caps. Soak the bean thread noodles in warm water to cover until softened, about 15 minutes; drain. Cut the noodles into 4-inch lengths. Combine the seasoning ingredients in a bowl.

Place a wok or wide frying pan over high heat until hot. Add the oil, swirling to coat the sides. Add the mushrooms, onion, carrot, celery, and noodles; stir-fry for 1 minute. Add the seasonings and cook, stirring, until the sauce is heated through. Place in a bowl and let cool.

Bring a pot of water to a boil. Add the cabbage leaves and cook until limp, about 2 minutes. Drain, rinse with cold running water, and drain again.

To stuff each leaf, place one-eighth of the filling across the stem end of the cabbage leaf. Fold in the sides over the filling, then roll up. Repeat with remaining leaves and filling.

Prepare a wok for steaming (see page 212). Place the vegetable pillows in a heatproof dish. Cover and steam over high heat for 15 minutes.

To serve, cut the pillows in half diagonally and arrange on a serving platter.

BABY BOK CHOY WITH STRAW MUSHROOMS

Size does matter, when it comes to picking baby bok choy. While smaller than regular bok choy, baby bok choy and Shanghai baby bok choy (with green stems) are much sweeter and less fibrous than the big ones and, hence, are a nice contrast in texture to the straw mushrooms.

Makes 4 servings

Seasonings

½ CUP CHICKEN STOCK

2 TABLESPOONS CHINESE RICE WINE OR
DRY SHERRY

1 TABLESPOON BLACK BEAN GARLIC
SAUCE

1 TEASPOON CHILE GARLIC SAUCE

• • •

2½ TABLESPOONS COOKING OIL

¼ TEASPOON SALT

10 OUNCES SHANGHAI BABY BOK CHOY,
CUT LENGTHWISE INTO QUARTERS

2 TEASPOONS FINELY CHOPPED GINGER

1 (8-OUNCE) CAN UNPEELED STRAW
MUSHROOMS, DRAINED

½ CUP SLICED WATER CHESTNUTS

¾ TEASPOON CORNSTARCH DISSOLVED
IN 1 TABLESPOON WATER

Combine the seasoning ingredients in a bowl.

Bring a pot of water to a boil. Add ½ tablespoon of the oil and the salt followed by the bok choy; cook until the bok choy is tender-crisp, 3 to 4 minutes. Drain, rinse with cold running water, and drain again. Arrange the bok choy on a serving platter; keep warm.

Place a wok or wide frying pan over high heat until hot. Add the remaining 2 tablespoons oil, swirling to coat the sides. Add the ginger and cook, stirring, until fragrant, about 10 seconds. Add the mushrooms and water chestnuts; stir-fry for 30 seconds. Add the seasonings and bring to a boil. Reduce the heat to medium-high and simmer for 3 to 4 minutes. Add the cornstarch mixture and cook, stirring, until the sauce boils and thickens. Pour the mushroom mixture over the bok choy.

Finding Gold in the Straw

Straw mushrooms have a delicate sweetness and a firm, meaty texture that goes well in simmered dishes and stews. They are available peeled or unpeeled, in cans and sometimes fresh. Most chefs prefer the unpeeled ones, which are more flavorful. If you use canned ones, make sure you drain the liquid from the can and rinse the mushrooms well before cooking them.

SPINACH WITH DEEP-FRIED GARLIC

Gilroy, a small town south of San Francisco, holds a renowned garlic festival each year. Garlic appears in more guises than you might imagine—even as garlic ice cream. Every time I roast garlic in my kitchen, I am reminded of Gilroy and the joys of garlic. The garlic in this dish will ensure that you enjoy eating your spinach.

Makes 4 servings

1 POUND SPINACH OR PEA SHOOTS

COOKING OIL FOR DEEP-FRYING

12 CLOVES GARLIC

12 SLICES PEELED GINGER

1 TEASPOON JULIENNED RED JALAPEÑO
   CHILE

1 TABLESPOON CHINESE RICE WINE OR
   DRY SHERRY

1 TEASPOON SUGAR

1/2 TEASPOON SALT

Wash the spinach and remove the tough stems.

In a wok, heat the oil for deep-frying to 375°. Deep-fry the garlic and ginger until the garlic turns golden brown, about 30 seconds. Remove and drain on paper towels.

Remove all but 1 tablespoon of oil from the wok. Add the garlic, ginger, and jalapeño; cook over high heat, stirring, until fragrant, about 10 seconds. Add the spinach and stir-fry for 1 minute. Add the rice wine, sugar, and salt. Reduce the heat to medium-high; cover and cook for 5 minutes. Discard the excess liquid and place on a serving platter.

SAUTÉED MUSHROOMS OVER SPINACH

What's better than a delicious dish of sautéed black mushrooms? A delicious dish of sautéed black and white mushrooms. When it comes to mushrooms, there is always room for more.

Makes 4 servings

14 TO 16 DRIED BLACK (SHIITAKE) MUSHROOMS

8 OUNCES WHITE BUTTON MUSHROOMS

1½ POUNDS SPINACH

Seasonings

¾ CUP CHICKEN STOCK

3 TABLESPOONS VEGETARIAN OYSTER SAUCE

1 TEASPOON SESAME OIL

1 TABLESPOON COOKING OIL

1 TABLESPOON FINELY CHOPPED SHALLOT

1 TEASPOON FINELY CHOPPED GARLIC

1 TSP CORNSTARCH DISSOLVED IN 2 TEASPOONS WATER

Just Add Water

Dried mushrooms (black and shiitake are the same) need to be rehydrated before cooking. Soak them in warm water to cover for about 15 minutes. Rinse off any grit. Trim and discard the thick stems. Real mushroom lovers might want to strain the soaking liquid through a coffee filter and save it to add extra flavor to stocks and sauces.

Soak the dried mushrooms in warm water to cover until softened, about 15 minutes; drain. Discard the stems and leave the caps whole. Cut the button mushrooms in half. Wash the spinach and remove the tough stems. Combine the seasoning ingredients in a bowl.

Bring a pot of water to a boil. Add the spinach and cook until wilted, about 2 minutes; drain. Arrange the spinach on a serving platter; keep warm.

Place a wok or wide frying pan over high heat. Add the oil, swirling to coat the sides. Add the shallot and garlic; cook, stirring, until fragrant, about 10 seconds. Add the mushrooms and stir-fry for 2 minutes. Add the seasonings and bring to a boil. Reduce the heat to medium-high and simmer for 10 minutes. Add the cornstarch mixture and cook, stirring, until the sauce boils and thickens. Pour the mushrooms over the spinach and serve.

VEGETABLE STIR-FRY 101

Early Chinese immigrants to North America were credited with having invented chop suey, which can be loosely translated as "assorted bits of leftovers." Here is a recipe to give you that immigrant "can-do" spirit and clean out your fridge at the same time.

Makes 4 servings

Sauce

¼ CUP CHICKEN STOCK

1 TABLESPOON DARK SOY SAUCE

1 TABLESPOON OYSTER SAUCE

1 TEASPOON SESAME OIL

• • •

1 TABLESPOON COOKING OIL

1 CARROT, THINLY SLICED DIAGONALLY

1 RED BELL PEPPER, SEEDED AND CUT
  INTO BITE-SIZE PIECES

½ ONION, CUT INTO 1-INCH PIECES

2 OUNCES BABY CORN

1 OUNCE BROCCOLI FLORETS

1 OUNCE CAULIFLOWER FLORETS

Combine the sauce ingredients in a bowl.

Place a wok or wide frying pan over high heat until hot. Add the oil, swirling to coat the sides. Add the carrot, bell pepper, onion, baby corn, broccoli, and cauliflower; stir-fry for 1 minute. Add the sauce and bring to a boil. Reduce the heat to medium-high; cover and cook for 3 minutes.

CURRIED POTATOES

I once read that you shouldn't make a curry if you are in a hurry. While most good curry dishes do take a bit of simmering time, this flavorful potato side dish takes only 20 minutes from start to serving.

Makes 4 servings

Seasonings

1 CUP CHICKEN STOCK

¼ CUP UNSWEETENED COCONUT MILK

2½ TABLESPOONS SOY SAUCE

1½ TABLESPOONS CURRY POWDER

2 TEASPOONS CHILE GARLIC SAUCE

1 TEASPOON SUGAR

½ TEASPOON CHINESE FIVE-SPICE
   POWDER

◆ ◆ ◆

2 TABLESPOONS COOKING OIL

½ ONION, CUT INTO ½-INCH PIECES

2 TEASPOONS FINELY CHOPPED GINGER

12 OUNCES SMALL RED POTATOES, CUT
   INTO QUARTERS

4 OUNCES FROZEN PEAS AND CARROTS,
   THAWED

¼ CUP DICED WATER CHESTNUTS

2 OUNCES SLICED BAMBOO SHOOTS

1 TEASPOON CORNSTARCH DISSOLVED IN
   2 TEASPOONS WATER

Combine the seasoning ingredients in a bowl.

Place a wok or wide frying pan over high heat until hot. Add the oil, swirling to coat the sides. Add the onion and ginger; cook, stirring, until the onion turns translucent, about 2 minutes. Add the potatoes and seasonings; bring to a boil. Reduce the heat to low and simmer until the potatoes are nearly tender, 10 to 15 minutes. Add the peas and carrots, water chestnuts, and bamboo shoots; cook for 3 minutes. Add the cornstarch mixture and cook, stirring, until the sauce boils and thickens.

Tofu is the more common name for soybean curd, a smooth and custard-like substance extracted from cooked soybeans. It is high in vegetable protein and calcium, low in fat (and without cholesterol) and neutrally bland in taste, which makes it an excellent accompaniment for a wide range of ingredients and seasonings.

Different textures and degrees of firmness add to tofu's flexibility. Firm tofu can be deep-fried, and the regular kind can be stir-fried and braised in a variety of dishes. Soft or silken tofu can be used for desserts.

Most egg dishes in the West are either fried or poached. In China, we pan-fry eggs to make Egg Foo Yung, stir-fry them with other ingredients, drizzle them into Egg Flower Soup, preserve and age them in salt and brine, and use thin slivers of omelet as garnishes. Many Chinese recipes also call for steam power, which is a healthy (not to mention delicious) way to prepare egg dishes.

I never put all my eggs in one basket. I put some of them in this cookbook!

CREAMY EGGS WITH SHRIMP

When served over a bed of steamed rice, this makes a popular one-dish meal in many Chinese restaurants. It's tasty and easy to make at home—perfect for a quick lunch or an easy dinner.

Makes 4 servings

Marinade

1 TEASPOON CORNSTARCH
1/4 TEASPOON SALT
1/8 TEASPOON WHITE PEPPER

• • •

8 OUNCES MEDIUM RAW SHRIMP, SHELLED AND DEVEINED
4 EGGS
2 TABLESPOONS MILK
1/2 TEASPOON SESAME OIL
1/4 TEASPOON SALT
1/8 TEASPOON WHITE PEPPER
3 TABLESPOONS COOKING OIL
1/2 RED BELL PEPPER, SEEDED AND DICED
2 OUNCES FROZEN PEAS, THAWED (OPTIONAL)
2 TABLESPOONS CHOPPED GREEN ONION

Combine the marinade ingredients in a bowl. Add the shrimp and stir to coat. Let stand for 15 minutes. Lightly beat the eggs, milk, sesame oil, salt, and pepper in a bowl; set aside.

Place a nonstick frying pan over high heat until hot. Add 1 tablespoon of the oil, swirling to coat the sides. Add the shrimp and stir-fry for 1 minute. Remove from the wok.

Add the remaining oil to the pan, swirling to coat the sides. Add the eggs and cook, stirring, until they are softly set. Return the shrimp to the pan and add the bell pepper, peas, and green onion; gently toss for 30 seconds.

CHAR SIU FOO YUNG

In Chinese, foo yung *means the beauty of a peony flower. A beautiful Chinese woman is one with the face of a peony. Follow this recipe closely and carefully; you don't want to end up with egg on your beautiful face!*

Makes 4 servings

3 EGGS

1 TEASPOON SESAME OIL

½ TEASPOON SALT

½ TEASPOON WHITE PEPPER

ABOUT 3 TABLESPOONS COOKING OIL

2 OUNCES JULIENNED CHINESE
    BARBECUED PORK *(CHAR SIU)*

¼ CUP JULIENNED CARROT

3 OUNCES FRESH MUNG BEAN SPROUTS

CILANTRO SPRIGS

Lightly beat the eggs, sesame oil, salt, and pepper in a bowl.

Place a nonstick frying pan over high heat until hot. Add 1 tablespoon of the oil, swirling to coat the sides. Add the barbecued pork and carrot; stir-fry for 1 minute. Add the bean sprouts and stir-fry for 30 seconds.

Push the vegetable mixture to one side of the pan. Add the remaining 2 tablespoons of oil to the pan, swirling to coat the sides. Add the egg mixture and cook without stirring. Spread the vegetable mixture back into the center of the pan. If the mixture starts to stick, add a teaspoon or two of oil. As the edges begin to set, lift with a spatula and shake or tilt the pan to let the eggs flow underneath. When the eggs no longer flow freely, turn the omelet over and brown lightly on the other side. Garnish with cilantro sprigs.

Egg-citement

Chinese chefs often use thin ribbons of cooked egg as a garnish. Beat 2 eggs with ⅛ teaspoon salt. Place a nonstick frying pan over medium heat. Add ¼ teaspoon cooking oil. Pour in half of the egg mixture and swirl the pan to cover the entire surface. Cook until the eggs are lightly browned on the bottom and set on top, about 1 minute. Turn the sheet over and cook for 5 seconds; slide out of pan. Repeat with the rest of the egg mixture. When the sheets are cool, cut into thin strips.

STEAMED EGGS WITH SEAFOOD

A real change of pace from sweet baked custard, this Chinese version is not a dessert but a main course with bits of shrimp in it. This is a very popular dish among Chinese children, but I will be the first to confess that it is still one of my all-time favorite comfort foods.

Makes 4 servings

2 OUNCES DRIED SCALLOPS (OPTIONAL)

4 EGGS

1¼ CUPS MILK

½ TEASPOON SALT

¼ TEASPOON WHITE PEPPER

2 OUNCES SMALL RAW SHRIMP, SHELLED, DEVEINED, AND CUT IN HALF HORIZONTALLY

1 TABLESPOON SOY SAUCE

½ TEASPOON SESAME OIL

1 TABLESPOON CHOPPED GREEN ONION

Soak the scallops in warm water to cover until softened, about 15 minutes; drain. Place in a pan and cover with water; bring to a boil over high heat. Reduce the heat to low and simmer for 15 minutes; drain and shred the scallops.

Lightly beat the eggs, milk, salt, and pepper in a bowl. Add the scallops and shrimp; mix well.

Prepare a wok for steaming (see page 212). Pour the egg mixture into a heatproof pie dish and cover with plastic wrap. Steam, covered, over medium-high heat until the custard jiggles only slightly when the dish is shaken gently, 12 to 15 minutes.

Combine the soy sauce and sesame oil in a bowl. Drizzle over the custard and sprinkle with the green onion.

Smooth as Custard

The secret to silky smooth egg custard is in the heat. To keep the eggs smooth and soft, cover them with plastic wrap, and steam them over medium-high heat, until the custard jiggles only slightly when the pan is shaken gently, 12 to 15 minutes. (The old doneness test, inserting a knife into the center of the custard and having it come out clean, occurs when the custard is on the way to being overcooked.)

SAVORY SEAFOOD TOFU

Soft (or silken) tofu is too delicate to be stir-fried without breaking up, but there is a way that you can use soft tofu in a stir-fry dish. Just stir-fry the other ingredients and serve them over soft tofu heated in the microwave.

Makes 4 to 6 servings

Marinade

2 TEASPOONS CORNSTARCH

1/4 TEASPOON SALT

1/8 TEASPOON WHITE PEPPER

• • •

6 OUNCES SMALL RAW SHRIMP, SHELLED
    AND DEVEINED

4 OUNCES SCALLOPS, CUT INTO
    QUARTERS IF LARGE

Seasonings

1/2 CUP CHICKEN STOCK

1 TABLESPOON DARK SOY SAUCE

1 TABLESPOON LIGHT SOY SAUCE

1 TABLESPOON CHINESE RICE WINE OR
    DRY SHERRY

• • •

14 OUNCES SOFT TOFU, DRAINED

2 TABLESPOONS COOKING OIL

2 TEASPOONS FINELY CHOPPED GARLIC

1 GREEN ONION, CUT INTO 2-INCH
    LENGTHS

1/2 RED JALAPEÑO CHILE, SLICED

1/2 TEASPOON CORNSTARCH DISSOLVED
    IN 1 TEASPOON WATER

Combine the marinade ingredients in a bowl. Add the shrimp and scallops; stir to coat. Let stand for 15 minutes. Combine the seasoning ingredients in a bowl; set aside.

Place the tofu in a microwave-safe serving dish. Place in the microwave and cook on high heat until heated through, 2 to 3 minutes. If desired, cut the tofu into cubes, leaving shape intact.

Place a wok or wide frying pan over high heat until hot. Add the oil, swirling to coat the sides. Add the garlic and cook, stirring, until fragrant, about 10 seconds. Add the shrimp, scallops, green onion, and jalapeño; stir-fry until the shrimp turn pink, about 2 minutes. Add the seasonings and bring to a boil. Add the cornstarch mixture and cook, stirring, until the sauce boils and thickens. Pour over the tofu.

FRIED TOFU WITH PEPPERY BEAN SAUCE

In the streets of Hong Kong, deep-fried tofu squares are sold as snacks to enjoy at all times of the day. They are typically dipped in a hoisin-based sweet sauce. This recipe with black bean sauce gives the dish a richer and more robust taste.

Makes 4 servings

14 OUNCES FIRM TOFU, DRAINED

Seasonings

½ CUP CHICKEN STOCK

1½ TABLESPOONS DARK SOY SAUCE

1½ TEASPOONS SUGAR

• • •

1 SMALL LEEK

1 OUNCE SMOKED HAM

COOKING OIL FOR DEEP-FRYING

2 EGGS, LIGHTLY BEATEN

CORNSTARCH

4 CLOVES GARLIC, THINLY SLICED

1 TEASPOON FINELY CHOPPED GINGER

2 RED JALAPEÑO CHILES, SLICED

1 TABLESPOON SALTED BLACK BEANS, RINSED AND LIGHTLY CRUSHED, OR 2 TEASPOONS BLACK BEAN GARLIC SAUCE

1 TEASPOON CORNSTARCH DISSOLVED IN 2 TSP WATER

Cut the tofu into ½- by 2- by 2-inch pieces. Combine the seasoning ingredients in a bowl.

Cut the leek in half lengthwise, then into ½-inch slices. Cut the ham into 1- by 1- by ⅛-inch slices.

In a wok, heat the oil for deep-frying to 375°. Dip the tofu in the eggs, drain briefly, then coat with cornstarch. Deep-fry the tofu, a batch at a time, until golden brown, about 2 minutes. Remove and drain on paper towels.

Remove all but 2 tablespoons of oil from the wok. Place over high heat until hot. Add the garlic and ginger and cook, stirring, until fragrant, about 10 seconds; add the jalapeños, black beans, leek, and ham and stir-fry for 1 minute. Add the seasonings and bring to a boil. Add the cornstarch mixture and cook, stirring, until the sauce boils and thickens. Add the tofu and toss to coat.

Dining Under the Stars

So many of Asia's best and most rewarding experiences are found at informal outdoor food stands. From the *dai pai dongs* in Hong Kong, to the hawker stalls in Singapore, Malaysia, and Indonesia, to the busiest lamb skewer stand in the ancient Chinese capital of Xian, street food is an integral part of the Asian culinary adventure.

TOFU WITH SNOW PEAS

Stir-fried snow peas are crispy and have a natural sweetness. These attributes provide an interesting contrast to tofu, and the combination of the two makes a most interesting vegetarian treat.

Makes 4 servings

4 DRIED BLACK (SHIITAKE) MUSHROOMS

1/3 CUP CHICKEN STOCK

3 TABLESPOONS SOY SAUCE

1 TEASPOON SESAME OIL

1/8 TEASPOON WHITE PEPPER

1 TABLESPOON COOKING OIL

4 OUNCES CHINESE SAUSAGES (*LOP CHEONG*), THINLY SLICED DIAGONALLY, OR SLICED HAM, CUT INTO 1-INCH PIECES

2 OUNCES SNOW PEAS, ENDS AND STRINGS REMOVED

14 OUNCES FIRM TOFU, DRAINED AND CUT INTO 1/2-INCH CUBES

1/2 TEASPOON CORNSTARCH DISSOLVED IN 1 TEASPOON WATER

1/4 CUP BASIL LEAVES

RED BELL PEPPER, SEEDED AND CUT INTO DIAMOND SHAPES

Soak the mushrooms in warm water to cover until softened, about 15 minutes; drain. Discard the stems and dice the caps. In a bowl, combine the chicken stock, soy sauce, sesame oil, and pepper.

Place a wok or wide frying pan over high heat until hot. Add the oil, swirling to coat the sides. Add the sausages; stir-fry for 30 seconds. Add the snow peas; stir-fry until the snow peas are tender-crisp, about 1 minute. Add the tofu and chicken stock mixture; bring to a boil. Add the cornstarch mixture and cook, stirring, until the sauce boils and thickens. Add the basil. Garnish with the bell pepper.

SHRIMP AND SCALLOP FILLED TOFU

Carving a hole in a piece of soft tofu is a feat best left to the garnish artists. Simply spread the shrimp mousse on one side of the tofu and it will stay in place throughout its steam bath.

Makes 4 servings

Dressing

1 TABLESPOON SOY SAUCE

½ TEASPOON SESAME OIL

⅛ TEASPOON WHITE PEPPER

Seafood Mousse

3 OUNCES MEDIUM RAW SHRIMP,
   SHELLED AND DEVEINED

2 OUNCES SCALLOPS

1 TABLESPOON FINELY CHOPPED BACON

½ EGG WHITE

2 TEASPOONS CORNSTARCH

1 TEASPOON CHINESE RICE WINE OR
   DRY SHERRY

1 TEASPOON SESAME OIL

¼ TEASPOON SALT

• • •

14 OUNCES SOFT TOFU, DRAINED

1 GREEN ONION, CHOPPED

2 TEASPOONS CHOPPED CILANTRO

Combine the dressing ingredients in a bowl; set aside.

In a food processor, pulse the seafood mousse ingredients until finely chopped. Place the mixture in a bowl and stir rapidly to incorporate air into the mixture.

Cut the tofu in half horizontally; cut each piece in half lengthwise, then crosswise, to make 8 equal-sized pieces. Lay the tofu pieces in a heatproof serving dish.

Prepare a wok for steaming (see page 212). Spread the mousse over each piece of tofu. Sprinkle with the green onion and cilantro. Cover and steam until the mousse turns pink, about 6 minutes. Remove the dish from the steamer; carefully pour off the cooking juices. Drizzle the dressing over the tofu and serve.

SHRIMP AND SCALLOP
FILLED TOFU

MY MOM'S TOMATO TOFU

My mother is a firm believer in the beauty of simple dishes. Tomato Tofu is one of her favorites, and no matter where in the world I find myself to be, I always associate this dish with her home cooking.

Makes 4 to 6 servings

Sauce

3 TABLESPOONS KETCHUP

2 TABLESPOONS WORCESTERSHIRE SAUCE

2 TABLESPOONS SOY SAUCE

2 TEASPOONS CHILE GARLIC SAUCE

1 TEASPOON SESAME OIL

1 TEASPOON CHILE OIL

1 TABLESPOON COOKING OIL

10 OUNCES TOMATOES, PEELED AND DICED

1/4 CUP CILANTRO LEAVES, COARSELY CHOPPED

2 TABLESPOONS CHOPPED CRYSTALLIZED GINGER

14 OUNCES SOFT TOFU, DRAINED AND CUT INTO 1-INCH CUBES

Combine the sauce ingredients in a bowl.

Place a wok or wide frying pan over high heat until hot. Add the oil, swirling to coat the sides. Add the tomatoes, cilantro, and crystallized ginger; cook, stirring, for 2 minutes. Add the sauce and tofu; bring to a boil. Reduce the heat to medium and simmer until the tofu is heated through, 2 to 3 minutes.

YIN YANG TOFU

Here is a dish for true tofu enthusiasts (and who wouldn't be one after a taste of this dish?). Firm and soft tofu, the yin and yang of the tofu universe, are served with different sauces that bring different flavors to the same dish.

Makes 4 to 6 servings

Yin Sauce

⅓ CUP CHICKEN STOCK

3 TABLESPOONS OYSTER SAUCE

2 TEASPOONS SESAME OIL

¼ TEASPOON WHITE PEPPER

Yang Sauce

3 TABLESPOONS WHITE VINEGAR

2 TABLESPOONS KETCHUP

1 TEASPOON SOY SAUCE

½ TEASPOON CHILE GARLIC SAUCE

½ TEASPOON SUGAR

• • •

2 TABLESPOONS COOKING OIL

14 OUNCES FIRM TOFU, DRAINED AND
CUT INTO ½-INCH CUBES

5 OUNCES WHITE BUTTON MUSHROOMS,
SLICED

2 TEASPOONS CORNSTARCH DISSOLVED
IN 1½ TABLESPOONS WATER

14 OUNCES SOFT TOFU, DRAINED AND
CUT INTO 1-INCH CUBES

2 OUNCES FROZEN PEAS, THAWED

¼ CUP SLICED WATER CHESTNUTS

Combine the ingredients for the yin and yang sauces in separate bowls.

Place a wok over high heat until hot. Add 1 tablespoon of the oil, swirling to coat the sides. Add the firm tofu, mushrooms, and yin sauce; bring to a boil. Reduce the heat to low; cover and simmer for 2 minutes. Add half of the cornstarch mixture and cook, stirring, until the sauce boils and thickens. Place on one side of a serving platter.

Wipe out the wok and place it over high heat until hot. Add the remaining oil, swirling to coat the sides. Add the soft tofu, peas, water chestnuts, and yang sauce; bring to a boil. Reduce the heat to low; cover and simmer for 2 minutes. Add the remaining cornstarch mixture and cook, stirring, until the sauce boils and thickens. Place on the other side of the serving platter.

Balance of Life

The ancient Chinese philosophy of yin and yang is very much a part of Chinese cuisine. In cooking as in life, the goal is to maintain harmony between these two opposites. Yin symbolizes soft, cool, moist foods such as winter melon, asparagus, or fish. Yang is the robust taste of chiles, ginger, red meat, and fried food. Yin and yang's essence is harmony of flavors, colors, and textures in each.

HAKKA-STYLE TOFU STEW

This slowly braised pot of tofu and seafood is a delicious clay-pot classic. The recipe originated with the Hakka people, a Northern Chinese clan that migrated to Southern China. Traditionally, the tofu is stuffed with shrimp; here they are added separately. Now the recipe has moved abroad to delight diners the world over.

Makes 4 servings

Marinade

1 TEASPOON CORNSTARCH

½ TEASPOON SESAME OIL

¼ TEASPOON SALT

⅛ TEASPOON WHITE PEPPER

• • •

4 OUNCES FIRM WHITE FISH FILLET, CUT INTO ½-INCH PIECES

4 OUNCES MEDIUM RAW SHRIMP, SHELLED, DEVEINED, AND DICED

16 SMALL DRIED BLACK (SHIITAKE) MUSHROOMS

1½ CUPS CHICKEN STOCK

14 OUNCES NAPA CABBAGE, CUT INTO 2-INCH PIECES

8 OUNCES FIRM TOFU, DRAINED AND CUT INTO 1-INCH CUBES

Combine the marinade ingredients in a bowl. Add the fish and shrimp; stir to coat. Let stand for 15 minutes. Soak the mushrooms in warm water to cover until softened, about 15 minutes; drain. Discard the stems and leave the caps whole.

In a pot, bring the stock to a boil over medium-high heat. Add the mushrooms, cabbage, and tofu; bring to a boil. Reduce the heat to medium and cook until the cabbage is tender-crisp, about 3 minutes. Add the fish and shrimp. Cook until the shrimp turn pink, 2 to 3 minutes.

A Guest In Your Own Home

The word Hakka literally means "a guest who has made his home here." The Hakka people are nomads who migrated from the north central plains of China to the east and southeast of the country. Today, Hakka communities (with their famous clay pots and salt-baked chicken; see page 134) are prominent along the South China coast and in Southeast Asia.

POACHED TOFU WITH DRIED SHRIMP AND GREEN ONIONS

Seeking an alternative side dish to the same old boiled vegetables or tossed salad? This light and flavorful poached tofu is a perfect choice.

Makes 4 servings

2 TABLESPOONS DRIED SHRIMP

Dressing

1½ TABLESPOONS SOY SAUCE

2 TEASPOONS HOISIN SAUCE

2 TEASPOONS SESAME OIL

1 TEASPOON CHILE OIL

• • •

14 OUNCES REGULAR OR SOFT TOFU, DRAINED

2 TEASPOONS COOKING OIL

2 TABLESPOONS CHOPPED UNSALTED ROASTED PEANUTS

2 TABLESPOONS CHOPPED SICHUAN PRESERVED VEGETABLE

2 TABLESPOONS CHOPPED GREEN ONION

SLICED RED JALAPEÑO CHILES

Soak the shrimp in warm water to cover for 20 minutes; drain. Coarsely chop the shrimp. Combine the dressing ingredients in a bowl. Cut the tofu into ¾- by 2- by 2½-inch pieces.

Place a wok or small frying pan over high heat until hot. Add the oil, swirling to coat the sides. Add the shrimp and stir-fry for 1 minute.

Bring a pot of water to a boil. Add the tofu and return to a boil. Reduce the heat to medium and cook for 2 minutes; drain.

Arrange the tofu on a shallow serving plate. Sprinkle the shrimp, peanuts, preserved vegetable, and green onion over the tofu. Drizzle the dressing over all and garnish with the chiles.

Rice or Shrimp

In Cantonese, dried shrimp are called *ha mei,* which literally means "shrimp rice." These are tiny shrimp that are preserved in brine, then sun-dried, creating a hard, brittle surface similar to that of grains of rice. Their pungent taste adds extra flavor to vegetables and soups, and to fillings for a variety of dim sum.

SICHUAN TOFU (MA PO TOFU)

Lovers of spicy food will have a great time with this classic dish from Sichuan province. Legend has it that it was invented by a ma po, *an old lady with a pockmarked face. Not a terribly appetizing image, but just as one can't judge a book by its cover, one shouldn't judge a dish by its name.*

Makes 4 to 6 servings

Sauce

½ CUP CHICKEN STOCK

1 TABLESPOON DARK SOY SAUCE

2 TEASPOONS SESAME OIL

1 TEASPOON CHILE GARLIC SAUCE

• • •

2 TABLESPOONS COOKING OIL

2 TEASPOONS FINELY CHOPPED GARLIC

6 SMALL DRIED RED CHILES

2 GREEN ONIONS, CUT INTO 2-INCH
   LENGTHS

1 TABLESPOON BLACK BEAN GARLIC
   SAUCE

8 OUNCES GROUND LEAN PORK

14 OUNCES SOFT OR REGULAR TOFU,
   DRAINED AND CUT INTO ½-INCH
   CUBES

2 OUNCES SLICED BAMBOO SHOOTS

1 TEASPOON CORNSTARCH DISSOLVED IN
   2 TEASPOONS WATER

CHOPPED GREEN ONIONS

Combine the sauce ingredients in a bowl.

Place a wok or wide frying pan over high heat until hot. Add the oil, swirling to coat the sides. Add the garlic, chiles, green onion pieces, and black bean garlic sauce; cook, stirring, until fragrant, about 10 seconds. Add the pork and stir-fry until browned and crumbly, about 1½ minutes. Add the tofu, bamboo shoots, and sauce; cover and cook for 2 minutes. Add the cornstarch mixture and cook, stirring, until the sauce boils and thickens. Place in a shallow serving bowl and garnish with the chopped green onions.

Wash Your Hands!

When handling or chopping chile peppers, remember what your mother told you time and time again: "Wash your hands!" The pepper oil on your hands can touch your eyes or face, causing an uncomfortable burning sensation.

SEAFOOD

When it comes to Chinese seafood, one word and only one word matters: fresh! Imagine, the word for seafood in Chinese literally means "freshness from the sea." While a Western definition for fresh seafood may include "fresh frozen" (a self-contradicting term, in my opinion), in Chinese cooking fresh seafood could only mean alive and swimming vigorously.

The love of live fresh seafood is not only Chinese but Asian. Everywhere I travel in Asia, I come across wet markets where live seafood is kept in tanks of water for the most discriminating shoppers. In Hong Kong, seafood lovers shop for their favorite fish, shrimp, squid, and clams right off fishing boats in Aberdeen or Sai Kung Village.

Whether you buy your seafood at the supermarket or from your neighborhood fish market, the following pages will give you plenty of recipes to impress your friends and family. With a steamed fish as an honored dinner guest, your other guests will be most appreciative.

FISH AND CHIPS CHINESE-STYLE

Fish and chips can do well with a Chinese makeover. Say farewell to the old vinegar bottle, marinate the fish in Chinese rice wine and ginger, and serve the fish and chips with spicy salt and sweet and sour sauce.

Makes 4 servings

Batter

2/3 CUP ALL-PURPOSE FLOUR

1 1/4 TEASPOONS BAKING POWDER

1 TEASPOON SUGAR

3/4 CUP WATER

2 TEASPOONS COOKING OIL

• • •

1 POUND FIRM WHITE FISH FILLET, ABOUT
　1 INCH THICK

Marinade

2 TABLESPOONS CHINESE RICE WINE OR
　DRY SHERRY

2 TEASPOONS CHOPPED CILANTRO

2 TEASPOONS FINELY CHOPPED GINGER

1/4 TEASPOON SALT

1/4 TEASPOON WHITE PEPPER

Spicy Salt

1/3 CUP SALT

1 TEASPOON GROUND CHILE

1/4 TEASPOON SICHUAN PEPPERCORNS

1/4 TEASPOON WHITE PEPPER

• • •

2 LARGE POTATOES, CUT INTO WEDGES

COOKING OIL FOR DEEP-FRYING

ALL-PURPOSE FLOUR

SWEET AND SOUR SAUCE

First make the batter: Combine the flour, baking powder, and sugar in a bowl. Gradually add the water; whisk until blended. Whisk in the oil. Let stand for 1 1/2 hours.

Cut the fish into strips about 1 inch wide. Combine the marinade ingredients in a bowl. Add the fish and stir to coat. Let stand for 15 minutes.

To make the spicy salt: In a small frying pan, stir the salt, ground chile, peppercorns, and pepper over medium-high heat, shaking the pan frequently, until fragrant, 2 to 3 minutes. Process in a spice grinder or blender until coarsely ground.

Place the potatoes in a colander and rinse with cold running water; drain. Pat dry with paper towels. In a wok, heat the oil for deep-frying to 375°. Deep-fry the potatoes, a batch at a time, until tender and golden brown, about 3 minutes. Remove and drain on paper towels.

Dust the fish with flour, then dip into the batter; shake to remove the excess. Deep-fry until golden brown, 1 to 2 minutes. Drain on paper towels.

Arrange the fish and chips on a serving platter. Serve with the spicy salt and sweet and sour sauce alongside.

WOK-BRAISED FISH WITH BEAN SAUCE

Get the best fish available in the market for this recipe. Remember that the emphasis of Chinese seafood is on the quality of the fish, not the category of the fish. If a whole fish is not available, try fish steaks or fish fillets.

Makes 4 to 6 servings

6 DRIED BLACK (SHIITAKE) MUSHROOMS
1 WHOLE FISH (1½ TO 2 POUNDS),
   CLEANED
½ TEASPOON SALT
¼ TEASPOON WHITE PEPPER
ALL-PURPOSE FLOUR

Seasonings

1 CUP CHICKEN STOCK
¼ CUP CHINESE RICE WINE OR
   DRY SHERRY
2 TABLESPOONS SWEET BEAN SAUCE OR
   HOISIN SAUCE
1 TABLESPOON DARK SOY SAUCE
1 TABLESPOON LIGHT SOY SAUCE
2 TEASPOONS SUGAR

3 TABLESPOONS COOKING OIL
3 TABLESPOONS SLICED SHALLOTS
¼ CUP CHOPPED SICHUAN PRESERVED
   VEGETABLE
1 TEASPOON CORNSTARCH DISSOLVED IN
   2 TEASPOONS WATER
JULIENNED GREEN ONIONS

Fresh Facts

A fresh fish has clear, not cloudy eyes, bright red gills, and no fishy odor. Poke the flesh. It should be firm, slightly bouncy, and not soft and mushy. Don't be shy about asking for what is fresh that day. A knowledgeable and helpful seafood salesman is the one who gets repeat business.

Soak the mushrooms in warm water to cover until softened, about 15 minutes; drain. Discard the stems and chop the caps.

Score the fish several times on each side. Sprinkle with the salt and pepper. Dust the inside and outside of the fish with flour; shake to remove the excess. Let stand for 10 minutes. Combine the seasoning ingredients in a bowl.

Place a wok or wide frying pan over medium-high heat until hot. Add 2 tablespoons of the oil, swirling to coat the sides. Add the fish; cover and cook until golden brown, about 2 minutes on each side. Remove the fish from the wok.

Add the remaining oil to the wok, swirling to coat the sides. Add the shallots and cook, stirring, until fragrant, about 10 seconds. Add the mushrooms and preserved vegetable; stir-fry for 1½ minutes. Add the seasonings and bring to a boil. Return the fish to the wok. Spoon the seasonings over the fish. Cover and simmer until the center of the fish turns opaque (cut to test), 10 to 12 minutes.

To serve, place the fish on a serving platter and keep warm. Add the cornstarch mixture to the wok and cook, stirring, until the sauce boils and thickens. Spoon the sauce over the fish and garnish with the green onions.

SWEET AND SOUR DRAGON FISH

You don't need to slay a dragon to get dragon fish. Just score a fish fillet with shallow diagonal cuts, and coat it with cornstarch before frying. The fish will puff up like the scales of a dragon.

Makes 4 servings

12 OUNCES FIRM WHITE FISH FILLET,
   SKIN ON

½ TEASPOON SALT

3 TABLESPOONS PINE NUTS

Sauce

⅓ CUP WATER

⅓ CUP SEASONED RICE VINEGAR

¼ CUP SUGAR

2 TEASPOONS CHILE GARLIC SAUCE

COOKING OIL FOR DEEP-FRYING

CORNSTARCH

1 EGG, LIGHTLY BEATEN

ALL-PURPOSE FLOUR

2 TABLESPOONS DICED GREEN BELL
   PEPPER

2 TABLESPOONS DICED RED BELL PEPPER

½ CUP CRUSHED PINEAPPLE

2 TEASPOONS CORNSTARCH DISSOLVED
   IN 1½ TABLESPOONS WATER

. . .

Score the flesh side of the fish fillet at a 45° angle, leaving skin intact. Sprinkle the salt over the fish. Let stand for 15 minutes. Preheat the oven to 350°. Spread the pine nuts in a shallow baking pan. Toast, shaking pan occasionally, until fragrant and golden brown, 5 to 10 minutes. Remove from pan. Combine the sauce ingredients in a bowl.

In a wok, heat the oil for deep-frying to 375°. Dust the fish with cornstarch; shake to remove the excess. Dip the fish in the egg, drain briefly, then coat with flour; shake to remove the excess. Hold the ends of the fillet with tongs to form a U shape with the skin on the inside; this exposes the cut segments of the fish in a pinecone effect. Deep-fry the fish until golden brown, about 10 minutes. Remove and drain on paper towels.

Remove all but 1 tablespoon of oil from the wok, swirling to coat the sides. Add the bell peppers; stir-fry for 30 seconds. Add the pineapple and sauce; bring to a boil. Add the cornstarch mixture and cook, stirring, until the sauce boils and thickens.

Pour half of the sauce on a serving platter. Place the fish on the sauce, then ladle the remaining sauce over the fish. Sprinkle with the pine nuts.

Hitting the Bottle

One of the most common excuses I hear from people who don't cook is, "But I have no time!" Making sweet and sour sauce requires only a few minutes, but if you're pressed, there's an even quicker solution: sauce in a bottle. I've found several sweet and sour sauces on store shelves that do the trick, and quite acceptably, too.

SHALLOW-FRIED SALMON CAKES

In the PFP days, that is pre–food processor, chefs and home cooks made fish cakes the old-fashioned way, with a cleaver and lots and lots of chopping motion. Today, all that hard labor is reduced to the touch of a button. Amazing! Fish cakes for breakfast, anyone?

Makes 4 servings

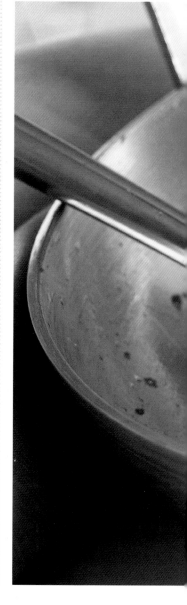

6 OUNCES SALMON FILLET, SKIN
   AND BONES REMOVED

4 OUNCES MEDIUM RAW SHRIMP,
   SHELLED AND DEVEINED

Seasonings

1 EGG WHITE, LIGHTLY BEATEN

1 TABLESPOON CHINESE RICE WINE OR
   DRY SHERRY

1 TABLESPOON OYSTER SAUCE

1 1/2 TABLESPOONS CORNSTARCH

1/2 TEASPOON SALT

1/4 TEASPOON WHITE PEPPER

* * *

1/3 CUP CHOPPED WATER CHESTNUTS

1 TABLESPOON CHOPPED CILANTRO

1 TABLESPOON CHOPPED GINGER

1 SLICE COOKED BACON, CRUMBLED

Sauce

1/2 CUP MAYONNAISE

1 TABLESPOON SESAME OIL

2 TEASPOONS OYSTER SAUCE

2 TEASPOONS SOY SAUCE

1 TEASPOON FINELY CHOPPED PICKLED
   GINGER

* * *

CORNSTARCH

1 EGG, LIGHTLY BEATEN

PANKO (JAPANESE BREAD CRUMBS)

4 TABLESPOONS COOKING OIL

Cut the salmon into chunks. Place the salmon and shrimp in a food processor; pulse until finely chopped. Add the seasoning ingredients and process until the mixture is smooth. Remove the salmon mixture to a bowl. Add the water chestnuts, cilantro, ginger, and bacon; mix well. Let stand for 15 minutes.

Combine the sauce ingredients in a bowl; mix well.

To make each cake, form about 2 ounces of the salmon mixture into a ball. Flatten with your palm into a cake about 1/2 inch thick. Dust with the cornstarch; shake to remove the excess. Dip in egg, drain briefly, then coat with the panko.

Place a wide frying pan over medium heat until hot. Add 2 tablespoons of the oil, swirling to coat the sides. Add half the cakes and cook until golden brown, 2 to 3 minutes on each side. Remove and drain on paper towels. Cook the remaining cakes with the remaining oil.

Arrange the cakes on a serving platter and serve with the sauce for dipping.

PAN-FRIED FISH WITH GINGERED WINE

Before deciding which wine to serve with dinner, let's settle on which wine to serve on dinner. For this recipe, I recommend Japanese sake or a Chinese rice wine (nonvintage). Cheers!

Makes 4 servings

½ OUNCE DRIED CLOUD EAR
   MUSHROOMS

12 OUNCES FIRM WHITE FISH FILLETS

1 TABLESPOON CORNSTARCH

¾ TEASPOON SALT

¼ TEASPOON WHITE PEPPER

2 TABLESPOONS COOKING OIL

2 TEASPOONS CORNSTARCH DISSOLVED
   IN 1½ TABLESPOONS WATER
   (OPTIONAL)

Sauce

½ CUP CHICKEN STOCK

½ CUP SAKE (JAPANESE RICE WINE) OR
   CHINESE RICE WINE

2 TABLESPOONS SOY SAUCE

1 TABLESPOON FINELY CHOPPED GINGER

1 TABLESPOON CHOPPED CRYSTALLIZED
   GINGER

1 TEASPOON SUGAR

Soak the mushrooms in warm water to cover until softened, about 15 minutes; drain. Cut into bite-size pieces.

Cut the fish into 3-inch pieces. Place the fish in a bowl and add the cornstarch, salt, and pepper; stir to coat. Let stand for 15 minutes. Combine the sauce ingredients in a bowl.

Place a wok or wide frying pan over high heat until hot. Add the oil, swirling to coat the sides. Add the fish and cook, turning once, until it turns golden brown, about 2 minutes on each side. Remove the fish from the wok.

Add the cloud ear mushrooms and stir-fry for 1 minute. Return the fish to the wok and add the sauce; bring to a boil. Reduce the heat to low and simmer for 5 minutes. If desired, add the cornstarch mixture and cook, stirring, until the sauce boils and thickens.

Listening to the Clouds

Cloud ears, tree ears, and wood ears are all dried black fungi that you can find in an Asian grocery. They look like chips of leather. Rehydrate them in warm water before using them in stir-fries or soups for texture and color contrast.

SIMMERED FISH WITH CHINKIANG VINEGAR

Simmering or poaching is a quick and easy alternative to steaming. Lest you have a preconceived notion that simmered food is bland and boring, the sweet and tangy sauce served on the fish will dispel that idea.

Makes 4 to 6 servings

Sauce

½ CUP CHINKIANG VINEGAR OR
   BALSAMIC VINEGAR

¼ CUP PACKED BROWN SUGAR

3 TABLESPOONS CHINESE RICE WINE OR
   DRY SHERRY

1 TABLESPOON DARK SOY SAUCE

1 TABLESPOON LIGHT SOY SAUCE

2 TEASPOONS JULIENNED GINGER

1 TEASPOON CORNSTARCH DISSOLVED IN
   2 TEASPOONS WATER

1 WHOLE FISH (1½ TO 2 POUNDS),
   CLEANED

6 SLICES GINGER, LIGHTLY CRUSHED

3 GREEN ONIONS, LIGHTLY CRUSHED

1 TEASPOON SALT

Combine the sauce ingredients in a pan. Bring to a boil over medium-high heat. Add the cornstarch mixture and cook, stirring, until the sauce boils and thickens. Keep warm.

Score the fish several times on each side.

Place the fish in a wok or frying pan and pour in enough water to partially cover the fish. Add the ginger slices, green onions, and salt; bring to a boil. Reduce the heat to low; cover and simmer until the fish turns opaque, about 10 minutes. Place the fish on a serving platter. Pour the sauce over the fish and serve.

Sour Power

For lighter color and flavor, I use Chinese or Japanese rice vinegar, but when the dish calls for a darker, more intense taste, I wheel out the big gun: Chinese black vinegar. It's made from fermented rice, wheat, and millet or sorghum, and has a distinctive smoky sweet flavor. A popular type of black vinegar produced in Eastern China is called Chinkiang vinegar. If you can't find black vinegar, balsamic vinegar is a great substitute; just cut down slightly on the sugar called for in the recipe to compensate. In addition to sauces, black vinegar is great in braised dishes or simply as a condiment for dumplings and hot and sour dishes.

STEAMED FISH FILLETS WITH GREEN ONIONS

Traditional Chinese cooking steams the whole fish, but more and more Chinese chefs are discovering the ease and joy of steaming fish fillets. Instead of having to clean and prepare a whole fish for the steamer, they can use the time gained to create a second dish.

Makes 4 to 6 servings

6 DRIED BLACK (SHIITAKE) MUSHROOMS

Sauce

½ CUP CHICKEN STOCK

⅓ CUP SOY SAUCE

3 TABLESPOONS CHINESE RICE WINE OR
   DRY SHERRY

2 TEASPOONS SUGAR

2 TEASPOONS CORNSTARCH DISSOLVED
   IN 1½ TABLESPOONS WATER

LETTUCE LEAVES

1½ POUNDS FIRM WHITE FISH FILLETS

4 SLICES GINGER, JULIENNED

2 GREEN ONIONS, JULIENNED

½ TEASPOON SALT

Soak the mushrooms in warm water to cover until softened, about 15 minutes; drain. Discard the stems and slice the caps.

Combine the sauce ingredients in a pan. Bring to a boil over medium-high heat. Add the cornstarch mixture and cook, stirring, until the sauce boils and thickens. Keep warm.

Prepare a wok for steaming (see page 212). Line a steamer basket with the lettuce leaves. Lay the fish over the lettuce, then top with the mushrooms, ginger, onions, and salt. Spoon about 3 tablespoons of the sauce over the fish. Place the steamer basket in the wok. Cover and steam until the fish turns opaque, 3 to 4 minutes.

To serve, place the fish on a serving platter. Serve with the remaining sauce.

A Fish Tale

The whole fish is used in Chinese cooking—bones, head, gills, fins, and all. They add flavor to the dish. There is, however, another reason for using the whole fish. Fish symbolizes abundance and fullness in Chinese culture. For this reason, whole fish is a must for any special banquet or Chinese New Year meals, and the head of the fish customarily points to the guest of honor.

WOK-SEARED SEA BASS WITH SEASONED SOY SAUCE

Don't panic if your kitchen doesn't have a wok sitting on the stove; use a large frying pan instead. Your guests will be equally impressed whether you serve them wok-seared or pan-seared sea bass.

Makes 4 servings

4 TEASPOONS CORNSTARCH

½ TEASPOON CHINESE FIVE-SPICE
   POWDER

½ TEASPOON SALT

½ TEASPOON WHITE PEPPER

1 POUND SEA BASS FILLETS, ABOUT
   1 INCH THICK

Sauce

½ CUP CHICKEN STOCK

¼ CUP LIGHT SOY SAUCE

2 TABLESPOONS DARK SOY SAUCE

4 TEASPOONS SUGAR

◆ ◆ ◆

3 TABLESPOONS COOKING OIL

NAPA CABBAGE LEAVES

Combine cornstarch, five-spice powder, salt, and pepper in a bowl. Sprinkle over the fish and let stand for 15 minutes.

Combine the sauce ingredients in a pan. Cook, stirring, until heated through. Keep warm.

Place a wok or wide frying pan over high heat until hot. Add the oil, swirling to coat the sides. Add the fish and cook, turning once, until golden brown, about 4 minutes on each side. Place the fish on a serving platter lined with the cabbage leaves. Pour the sauce over the fish and serve.

VELVET SHRIMP WITH CARAMELIZED NUTS

The use of mayonnaise is a fairly new practice in Chinese cooking. As the saying goes, we know a good thing when we see one. Shrimp with Caramelized Nuts is quickly becoming a classic in Chinese restaurants around the world.

Makes 4 servings

12 OUNCES MEDIUM RAW SHRIMP, SHELLED AND DEVEINED
2 TEASPOONS CORNSTARCH
¼ TEASPOON SALT

Sauce

½ CUP MAYONNAISE
2 TEASPOONS HONEY
2 TEASPOONS SOY SAUCE

5 TABLESPOONS COOKING OIL
3 TABLESPOONS SUGAR
¼ TEASPOON CHINESE FIVE-SPICE POWDER
1 CUP WALNUTS OR WHOLE CASHEWS

In a bowl, combine the shrimp, cornstarch, and salt; stir to coat. Let stand for 15 minutes. Combine the sauce ingredients in a bowl.

Place a pan over medium-high heat until hot. Add 3 tablespoons of the oil, swirling to coat the sides. Add the sugar and cook, stirring, until the sugar dissolves. Add the five-spice powder and mix well. Add the walnuts and turn to coat with the oil and sugar. Place on a baking sheet lined with parchment paper. With a fork, separate the nuts and let them cool.

Place a wok or wide frying pan over high heat until hot. Add the remaining oil, swirling to coat the sides. Add the shrimp and stir-fry until they turn pink, about 1½ minutes. Remove the wok from the heat. Add the sauce and toss to coat. Place the shrimp on a serving platter and sprinkle with the nuts.

Dry-Braised Shrimp

The bold and robust taste of black beans reaches new heights when combined with garlic, chile, and a dash of ketchup. Your tastebuds are in for a treat with this most interesting recipe.

Makes 4 servings

12 OUNCES MEDIUM RAW SHRIMP,
   SHELLED AND DEVEINED

2 TEASPOONS CORNSTARCH

¼ TEASPOON SALT

2 TABLESPOONS COOKING OIL

2 TEASPOONS FINELY CHOPPED GARLIC

1 TEASPOON SALTED BLACK BEANS,
   RINSED AND LIGHTLY CRUSHED

¼ CUP KETCHUP

2 TEASPOONS CHILE GARLIC SAUCE

1 TEASPOON SESAME OIL

½ TEASPOON SUGAR

LETTUCE CUPS

Combine the shrimp, cornstarch, and salt in a bowl; stir to coat. Let stand for 15 minutes.

Place a wok or wide frying pan over high heat until hot. Add the oil, swirling to coat the sides. Add the garlic and black beans; cook, stirring, until fragrant, about 10 seconds. Add the shrimp and stir-fry until they turn pink, about 1½ minutes. Add the ketchup, chile garlic sauce, sesame oil, and sugar; cook, stirring, until the sauce is heated through. Place on a serving platter; spoon into lettuce cups to eat.

The Shell Game

In Chinese cooking, shrimp shells are often left on throughout the cooking process to give the dish extra flavor. Shells that have been discarded before cooking are saved for enriching seafood soup stock.

KUNG PAO SHRIMP

This dish, a cousin of the famous Sichuan Kung Pao Chicken, packs a fiery punch: hot, sour, sweet, and savory. Pow!

Makes 4 servings

12 OUNCES MEDIUM RAW SHRIMP, SHELLED AND DEVEINED

2 TEASPOONS CORNSTARCH

1/2 TEASPOON SALT

1/4 TEASPOON WHITE PEPPER

2 TABLESPOONS COOKING OIL

1/2 ONION, CUT INTO 1/2-INCH SQUARES

1 SMALL RED JALAPEÑO CHILE, SLICED

2 OUNCES DICED BAMBOO SHOOTS

1/2 CUP UNSALTED ROASTED PEANUTS

Sauce

1/2 TEASPOON SICHUAN PEPPERCORNS

2 TABLESPOONS RICE VINEGAR

2 TABLESPOONS HOISIN SAUCE

1 TABLESPOON DARK SOY SAUCE

1/2 TEASPOON DRIED RED PEPPER FLAKES

In a bowl, combine the shrimp, cornstarch, salt, and pepper. Stir to coat. Let stand for 15 minutes.

Place the peppercorns in a small frying pan over medium heat. Cook, shaking the pan frequently, until the peppercorns darken slightly and smell toasted, 3 to 4 minutes. Process in a spice grinder or blender until coarsely ground. In a bowl, combine the peppercorns, vinegar, hoisin sauce, soy sauce, and pepper flakes.

Place a wok or wide frying pan over high heat until hot. Add the oil, swirling to coat the sides. Add the shrimp and stir-fry until they turn pink, about 1 1/2 minutes. Add the onion, jalapeño, and bamboo shoots; stir-fry for 1 minute. Add the sauce and cook until heated through. Add the peanuts and toss to coat.

SNOW PEAS WITH WINE-FLAVORED SHRIMP

Stir-fried snow peas are sweet and crunchy and their jade green color provides a dramatic contrast to the freshly cooked pink shrimp. This dish tastes as wonderful as it looks.

Makes 4 servings

8 OUNCES MEDIUM RAW SHRIMP,
    SHELLED AND DEVEINED, WITH TAILS
    INTACT
1 TEASPOON CORNSTARCH
1 TEASPOON SALT

Sauce

⅓ CUP CHICKEN STOCK
3 TABLESPOONS CHINESE RICE WINE OR
    DRY SHERRY
1 TEASPOON SUGAR
½ TEASPOON CORNSTARCH
½ TEASPOON SALT

1 RED JALAPEÑO CHILE
8 OUNCES SNOW PEAS
4 OUNCES BABY CORN
2 OUNCES FRESH SHIITAKE MUSHROOMS
1 TABLESPOON COOKING OIL
2 TABLESPOONS MINT LEAVES
1 TEASPOON FINELY CHOPPED GARLIC

In a bowl, combine the shrimp, cornstarch, and salt. Stir to coat. Let stand for 15 minutes. Combine the sauce ingredients in a bowl.

Cut the jalapeño in half lengthwise. Discard the seeds, then julienne. Remove the ends and strings from the snow peas. Cut the corn in half diagonally. Stem and slice the mushrooms.

Place a wok or wide frying pan over high heat until hot. Add the oil, swirling to coat the sides. Add the jalapeño, mint, and garlic; cook, stirring, until fragrant, about 10 seconds. Add the shrimp and stir-fry for 1½ minutes. Add the snow peas, corn, and mushrooms; stir-fry until the snow peas are tender-crisp, about 1 minute. Add the sauce and cook, stirring, until the sauce boils and thickens.

Peas' Cues

Sugar snap peas and snow peas are edible pea pods, and they both have a sweet, sugary taste. Crisp and crunchy when raw, they are terrific in a quick stir-fry because they cook up in no time. At the market, buy only the freshest, greenest peas with unblemished skins. If you grow your own, you're lucky: you can pick them at their peak.

CLAMS WITH BASIL AND CHILES

Ready to "open up" to a new clam recipe? Combining fresh basil with red and green jalapeño chiles gives this dish an exciting and unusual punch. A grand slam of a clam dish!

Makes 4 to 6 servings

2 POUNDS SMALL HARD-SHELL CLAMS,
    WELL SCRUBBED

Sauce

1/3 CUP CHICKEN STOCK

2 TABLESPOONS CHINESE RICE WINE OR
    DRY SHERRY

2 TEASPOONS DARK SOY SAUCE

2 TEASPOONS SESAME OIL

1 TEASPOON SUGAR

1 TEASPOON CORNSTARCH

1 TABLESPOON COOKING OIL

1 GREEN JALAPEÑO CHILE, THINLY
    SLICED

1 RED JALAPEÑO CHILE, THINLY SLICED

1 TABLESPOON FINELY CHOPPED GARLIC

1/2 ONION, CUT INTO 1/2-INCH SQUARES

1/4 CUP FRESH BASIL LEAVES

Happy as a Clam

Remember to discard any clams whose shells do not open during cooking. A happy clam is a smiling (wide open) clam.

Bring a pot of water to a boil. Add the clams and cook until they open, about 1 1/2 minutes; drain. Combine the sauce ingredients in a bowl.

Place a wok or wide frying pan over high heat until hot. Add the oil, swirling to coat the sides. Add the green and red jalapeños and garlic; cook, stirring, until fragrant, about 30 seconds. Add the onion and stir-fry for 1 minute. Add the clams, sauce, and basil; cook, stirring, until the sauce boils and thickens.

FRESH SHELLFISH, SUCH AS SEA SNAILS, ARE AVAILABLE IN CHINATOWN FISH MARKETS AND CAN BE USED INSTEAD OF CLAMS.

SOUTH CHINA SEA SPICY CRAB

In my travels to many parts of Southeast Asia, I have come upon different versions of spicy crab. Here I have combined the best elements to make an exciting treat for all you crab lovers.

Makes 4 servings

4 LIVE BLUE CRABS, OR 1 LIVE
    DUNGENESS CRAB (ABOUT 1½
    POUNDS), WELL SCRUBBED
1 TEASPOON SALT

Sauce

1 CUP CHICKEN STOCK
⅓ CUP KETCHUP
¼ CUP CHINESE RICE WINE OR DRY
    SHERRY
3 TABLESPOONS SWEET CHILE SAUCE
2 TABLESPOONS SOY SAUCE

COOKING OIL FOR DEEP-FRYING
ALL-PURPOSE FLOUR
3 TABLESPOONS CHOPPED GINGER
3 GREEN ONIONS, SLICED
1 TABLESPOON MINT LEAVES

Bring a pot of water to a boil. Add the crabs and cook until the shells turn bright red, about 2 minutes. Drain, rinse with cold running water, and drain again.

Twist off the crab claws and legs. Lightly crack the shells. Pull off and discard the bottom shell. Discard the gills and innards. Cut the crab bodies in half; if using Dungeness crab, cut the body into 6 pieces. Place the crab claws, legs, and body pieces in a bowl. Add the salt and stir to coat.

Combine the sauce ingredients in a bowl.

In a wok, heat the oil for deep-frying to 375°. Dust the crab with flour; shake to remove the excess. Deep-fry the crab, several pieces at a time, until golden brown, 3 to 4 minutes. Remove and drain on paper towels.

Remove all but 2 tablespoons of oil from the wok, swirling to coat the sides. Add the ginger, green onions, and mint; stir-fry for 2 minutes. Add the crab and sauce; bring to a boil. Reduce the heat to low; cover and simmer, 8 to 10 minutes. To reduce and thicken the sauce, uncover and cook for 1 minute.

Feeling Crabby?

To real crab lovers, there is no substitute for live crabs. Be aware that live crabs do not keep well. Try to cook them on the day of purchase. Many markets will also clean and prepare the crab for you, thereby saving you the agony of running after live critters across your kitchen floor.

Twin Seafood with Broccoli

The shrimp and scallops of this dynamic seafood duo might not look like twins, but when it comes to taste, they are identically wonderful.

Makes 4 to 6 servings

Marinade

1 TEASPOON CORNSTARCH

¼ TEASPOON SALT

⅛ TEASPOON WHITE PEPPER

· · ·

8 OUNCES MEDIUM RAW SHRIMP,
 SHELLED AND DEVEINED

4 OUNCES SCALLOPS, CUT IN HALF
 HORIZONTALLY

Sauce

⅓ CUP CHICKEN STOCK

2 TABLESPOONS CHINESE RICE WINE OR
 DRY SHERRY

2 TABLESPOONS OYSTER SAUCE

· · ·

10 OUNCES BROCCOLI FLORETS

2 TABLESPOONS COOKING OIL

2 TEASPOONS FINELY CHOPPED GINGER

½ CUP SLICED WATER CHESTNUTS

2 OUNCES STRAW MUSHROOMS

2 TEASPOONS CORNSTARCH DISSOLVED
 IN 4 TEASPOONS WATER

Combine the marinade ingredients in a bowl. Add the shrimp and scallops; stir to coat. Let stand for 15 minutes. Combine the sauce ingredients in a bowl.

Bring a pot of water to a boil. Add the broccoli and cook until tender-crisp, about 2 minutes; drain.

Place a wok or wide frying pan over high heat until hot. Add the oil, swirling to coat the sides. Add the ginger and cook, stirring, until fragrant, about 10 seconds. Add the shrimp and scallops; stir-fry until the shrimp turn pink, about 1½ minutes. Add the broccoli, water chestnuts, and mushrooms; mix well. Add the sauce and bring to a boil. Add the cornstarch mixture and cook, stirring, until the sauce boils and thickens.

No Vein, No Pain
Deveining shrimp is easier than it looks. Remove the legs and shell, then run a sharp paring knife along the back of the shrimp to expose the "vein," which is actually the intestine. Remove the vein with the tip of the knife, and rinse the shrimp quickly under cold running water. Pat shrimp dry before marinating.

FIVE-SPICE FRIED SQUID

You can call it calamari or you can call it squid, but if you deep-fry it and serve it with five-spice salt, make sure you call me for dinner.

Makes 4 servings

12 OUNCES SMALL SQUID, CLEANED

1/8 TEASPOON SALT

1/8 TEASPOON WHITE PEPPER

COOKING OIL FOR DEEP-FRYING

3 TABLESPOONS CHOPPED GINGER

3 GREEN ONIONS, CUT INTO 1-INCH LENGTHS

2 RED JALAPEÑO CHILES, SEEDED AND JULIENNED

1 TEASPOON SPICED SALT (SEE PAGE 128)

Leave the squid tentacles whole. Cut the bodies open and lightly score the inner side in a small crisscross pattern. Cut the body into 1½- by 2-inch pieces. Place the squid in a bowl and add the salt and pepper; stir to coat. Let stand for 15 minutes.

In a wok, heat the oil for deep-frying to 375°. Deep-fry the squid, half at a time, until tender, about 1 minute. Remove and drain on paper towels.

Remove all but 1 tablespoon of oil from the wok, swirling to coat the sides. Add the ginger, green onions, and jalapeños; stir-fry for 2 minutes. Add the squid and stir-fry for 1 to 2 minutes. Add the spiced salt and toss to coat.

No Moderation

Squid cooking is a case of extremes. Either you cook it briefly, deep-fry for 1 minute as in the recipe here, or for a long time, in the case of a seafood stew, for example. Squid tastes tough and rubbery if you cook it for any time frame in between.

CANTONESE-STYLE MUSSELS

Black bean sauce is popular in Southern China, a region that is blessed with some of the best seafood anywhere. It is therefore only natural that the two combine to create a culinary delight.

Makes 4 servings

1 1/2 POUNDS MUSSELS, WELL SCRUBBED
  AND BEARDS REMOVED

Sauce

1/2 CUP CHICKEN STOCK

3 TABLESPOONS CHINESE RICE WINE OR
  DRY SHERRY

2 TABLESPOONS SALTED BLACK BEANS,
  RINSED AND CRUSHED

1 TABLESPOON DARK SOY SAUCE

1 TEASPOON CORNSTARCH

1/2 TEASPOON SUGAR

2 1/2 TABLESPOONS COOKING OIL

3 CLOVES GARLIC, SLICED

1 TEASPOON DRIED RED PEPPER FLAKES

1 GREEN ONION, THINLY SLICED

2 TEASPOONS CORNSTARCH DISSOLVED
  IN 1 TABLESPOON WATER

1/2 TEASPOON SESAME OIL

Prepare a wok for steaming (see page 212). Place the mussels in a heatproof dish. Cover and steam the mussels over high heat until the shells open, 4 to 5 minutes. Let cool. Reserve 1/2 cup of the mussel steaming liquid; discard sandy residue.

Combine the sauce ingredients in a bowl.

Place a wok over high heat until hot. Add the oil, swirling to coat the sides. Add the garlic, pepper flakes, and green onion; cook, stirring, until fragrant, about 10 seconds. Add the mussels, the reserved mussel steaming liquid, and sauce; bring to a boil. Add the cornstarch mixture and cook, stirring, until the sauce boils and thickens. Stir in the sesame oil.

Mussel Bound

When shopping for mussels, make sure that they are closed tightly or close quickly the moment you pick them up. If the two halves of the shell slide back and forth, the mussel is dead and therefore unfit for eating. During cooking, mussels should open up like clams. Discard any that remain closed.

When it comes to putting our fine-feathered friends on the menu, my motto has always been: Fowl play is fair play! In China, there is precious little space for cattle farming; chickens, ducks, and geese are more economical sources of food.

After five thousand years of trials (and errors), we probably have as many ways to cook chicken as there are chickens in China. We poach them, stir-fry them, deep-fry them, braise them, put them in soup, steam them, red-cook them, smoke them, put them in salad, and, yes, on occasion we even bake them. Every regional cuisine boasts a classic chicken recipe. I have included some of these classics in this chapter, with minor modifications for taste, saving time, and availability of ingredients.

Start with the simple dishes like Chicken with Roasted Cashew Nuts and Soy Sauce Chicken, then graduate to the more exotic Pineapple Ginger Duck and Spiced Poussins with Sizzling Oil. Go ahead, be bold, and enjoy yourself like a true chef, or are you . . . chicken?

SPICY CHICKEN DRUMSTICKS

Looking for ways to get more mileage out of chicken? Spice up some legs! Follow this recipe, and watch how quickly they march into your dining room.

Makes 2 to 4 servings

Marinade

2 TABLESPOONS CHINESE RICE WINE OR
   DRY SHERRY

2 TABLESPOONS SOY SAUCE

2 TABLESPOONS CORNSTARCH

2 TABLESPOONS FINELY CHOPPED
   GREEN ONION

1 TABLESPOON GRATED GINGER

◆ ◆ ◆

4 CHICKEN DRUMSTICKS

Spiced Salt

2 TEASPOONS SALT

1 TEASPOON CHINESE FIVE-SPICE
   POWDER

¼ TEASPOON WHITE PEPPER

◆ ◆ ◆

COOKING OIL FOR DEEP-FRYING

CORNSTARCH

Combine the marinade ingredients in a bowl. Add the chicken and stir to coat. Cover and refrigerate for 1 to 2 hours.

Combine the spiced salt ingredients in a frying pan. Cook, stirring, over low heat, until toasted and fragrant, about 2 minutes. Place in a bowl.

In a wok, heat the oil for deep-frying to 300°. Dust the chicken with cornstarch; shake to remove the excess. Deep-fry the chicken for 2 minutes. Increase the heat to 325°. Continue cooking, turning occasionally, until the meat is no longer pink when cut near the bone, 8 to 10 minutes. Remove and drain on paper towels.

Place the chicken on a serving platter. Serve with the spiced salt.

Turn Up the Heat

Two important things to remember about deep-frying drumsticks: start at a lower temperature, then increase the heat as the frying process continues. This will prevent the outside of the drumsticks from burning before the inside is properly cooked.

DICED CHICKEN IN LETTUCE WRAP

There is nothing dicey about filling lettuce leaves with chicken. This classic dish is a popular choice for an appetizer as well as an entrée. It is elegant yet simple: prepare the chicken, the vegetables, and, as they say in the television cooking show business . . . it's a wrap!

Makes 6 servings

8 OUNCES BONELESS, SKINLESS CHICKEN, SQUAB, OR PORK, CUT INTO ¼-INCH CUBES

1 TABLESPOON OYSTER SAUCE OR STIR-FRY SAUCE

1 TABLESPOON COOKING OIL

1 RED BELL PEPPER, CUT INTO ¼-INCH CUBES

1 ZUCCHINI, CUT INTO ¼-INCH CUBES

6 WHITE BUTTON MUSHROOMS, DICED

8 OUNCES DICED BAMBOO SHOOTS

3 TABLESPOONS HOISIN SAUCE

12 SMALL ICEBERG LETTUCE LEAVES

Place the chicken in a bowl and add the oyster sauce; stir to coat. Let stand for 15 minutes.

Place a wok or wide frying pan over high heat until hot. Add the oil, swirling to coat the sides. Add the chicken and stir-fry for 2 minutes. Add the bell pepper, zucchini, mushrooms, and bamboo shoots; stir-fry for 2 minutes. If the mixture appears dry, add a tablespoon or two of water. Add the hoisin sauce and cook until heated through.

To eat, spread a heaped spoonful of the meat mixture in a lettuce leaf. Wrap up and eat with your fingers.

Dice Is Nice

Dicing chicken, duck, shrimp, and vegetables makes it a sure bet that the dish they go into will cook up quickly, with all the cubes nicely coated with sauce and the texture firm but not hard to the bite.

CHICKEN WINGS WITH BAMBOO SHOOTS AND CHESTNUTS

On a wintry night, nothing warms my heart and my appetite quite like a stew simmering on the stove. In my youth, we used traditional Chinese clay pots, but any flameproof pot will work.

Makes 4 to 6 servings

3½ OUNCES DRIED CHESTNUTS

5 DRIED BLACK (SHIITAKE) MUSHROOMS

1½ POUNDS CHICKEN WINGS

2 TABLESPOONS COOKING OIL

4 SLICES GINGER, LIGHTLY CRUSHED

4 WALNUT-SIZED SHALLOTS, QUARTERED

4 OUNCES WHOLE BAMBOO SHOOTS, CUT INTO BITE-SIZE PIECES

⅓ CUP CHINESE RICE WINE OR DRY SHERRY

¼ CUP SLICED WATER CHESTNUTS

⅓ CUP DARK SOY SAUCE

3 TABLESPOONS LIGHT SOY SAUCE

2 TABLESPOONS PACKED BROWN SUGAR

Soak the dried chestnuts overnight in water to cover; drain. Place in a pan and cover with water. Simmer, covered, until soft, about 45 minutes; drain. Soak the mushrooms in warm water to cover until softened, about 15 minutes. Reserve the mushroom soaking liquid. Discard the stems and cut the caps into quarters. Cut the chicken wings at the joints; reserve the bony tips for other uses or discard.

Place a wok over medium-high heat until hot. Add the oil, swirling to coat the sides. Add the chicken, ginger, and shallots. Cook until the chicken is browned on all sides, about 4 minutes.

In a large pot, add the reserved mushroom soaking liquid and enough water to make 2½ cups. Add the soaked dried chestnuts, bamboo shoots, rice wine, water chestnuts, soy sauces, and brown sugar; bring to a boil over high heat. Reduce the heat to low and simmer for 10 minutes. Add the chicken, ginger, and shallots; cover and simmer until the chicken and chestnuts are tender, about 30 minutes.

Your Own Pot-folio

For centuries, clay pots (or sand pots, because they are made from a mixture of sand and clay) have been occupying a prominent position in the Chinese kitchen. They're glazed on the inside but not the outside, and come with heavy lids that are often protected by a cage of metal wires. The pots also come in many different sizes and are both functional for cooking and attractive for serving a soup or a braised dish right at the table.

The General's Spicy Chicken

Tsao was a general from Hunan province better known to cooks for his taste for poultry than his military genius. Historians might have a different opinion, but even they can agree that this chicken dish will bring peace around the dining table.

<u>Makes 4 servings</u>

Marinade

2 TABLESPOONS SOY SAUCE

2 TEASPOONS CORNSTARCH

· · ·

12 OUNCES BONELESS, SKINLESS
    CHICKEN BREASTS, CUT INTO ¾-INCH
    PIECES

Sauce

2 TABLESPOONS HOISIN SAUCE

2 TABLESPOONS RICE VINEGAR

2 TABLESPOONS WATER

1½ TABLESPOONS LIGHT SOY SAUCE

2 TEASPOONS SESAME OIL

2 TEASPOONS SUGAR

1½ TEASPOONS HOT PEPPER SAUCE

· · ·

2 TABLESPOONS COOKING OIL

10 SMALL DRIED RED CHILES

2 TEASPOONS FINELY CHOPPED GARLIC

3 GREEN ONIONS, CUT INTO
    1-INCH PIECES

Chile Madness?

Ten chiles in one dish? Sounds excessive, but it isn't really, if you stir-fry them whole, because chiles' heat comes from the seeds within. The chiles are in this dish for their flavor and color, and, of course, to add a touch of heat. Just remember not to bite into one unless you are ready for a close encounter of the burning hot kind.

Combine the marinade ingredients in a bowl. Add the chicken and stir to coat. Let stand for 15 minutes. Combine the sauce ingredients in a bowl.

Place a wok or wide frying pan over high heat until hot. Add the oil, swirling to coat the sides. Add the chiles and cook, stirring, until fragrant, about 10 seconds. Add the chicken and garlic; stir-fry for 2 minutes. Add the onions and sauce; cook until the sauce thickens, 2 to 3 minutes. Continue cooking to caramelize or until all pieces are well coated, about 1 minute.

CHICKEN WITH ROASTED CASHEW NUTS

I don't know a single Chinese restaurant that doesn't have this dish on their menu. This popular dish is also easy to make at home. Of course you can use any kind of roasted nuts.

Makes 4 servings

Marinade

1 TABLESPOON OYSTER SAUCE
1/4 TEASPOON WHITE PEPPER

* * *

12 OUNCES BONELESS, SKINLESS CHICKEN BREASTS, CUT INTO 1/2-INCH CUBES
2 TABLESPOONS COOKING OIL
2 TEASPOONS FINELY CHOPPED GARLIC
4 OUNCES ASPARAGUS, TRIMMED AND CUT INTO 1-INCH PIECES
1 SMALL CARROT, THINLY SLICED
1/2 CUP CHICKEN STOCK
3/4 CUP SLICED WATER CHESTNUTS
1 TABLESPOON CHINESE RICE WINE OR DRY SHERRY
1 TEASPOON CORNSTARCH DISSOLVED IN 2 TEASPOONS WATER
2/3 CUP ROASTED CASHEWS

Pick the Season

Don't worry if your favorite vegetable is out of season. Choose whatever looks best and is in season locally. If asparagus is out, no problem. Use sugar snap peas, snow peas, or green beans instead. One important thing to remember about Chinese cooking is to take advantage of whatever is in season, and don't be shy about trying something new.

Combine the marinade ingredients in a bowl. Add the chicken and stir to coat. Let stand for 15 minutes.

Place a wok or wide frying pan over high heat until hot. Add the oil, swirling to coat the sides. Add the chicken and garlic; stir-fry for 2 minutes. Add the asparagus, carrot, and stock. Cook until the vegetables are tender-crisp, about 3 minutes. Add the water chestnuts and rice wine; cook for 1 minute. Add the cornstarch mixture and cook, stirring, until the sauce boils and thickens. Add the cashews and toss to coat.

CHICKEN WITH ROASTED CASHEW NUTS

SALT-BAKED CHICKEN

Here is a cooking tip you might think you had to take with more than a few grains of salt—2½ cups of kosher salt, to be exact. Don't worry, the salt will come off before you serve the chicken, but the bird's flavor is nicely baked in.

Makes 6 servings

Seasonings

1 ONION, COARSELY CHOPPED

2 TABLESPOONS SOY SAUCE

1 TABLESPOON FINELY CHOPPED GINGER

1 TABLESPOON CHINESE RICE WINE OR
  DRY SHERRY

½ TEASPOON CHINESE FIVE-SPICE
  POWDER

½ TEASPOON SALT

1 WHOLE FRYING CHICKEN (3 TO
  3½ POUNDS)

2½ CUPS KOSHER SALT

½ CUP WATER

Combine the seasoning ingredients in a bowl.

Remove the chicken neck and giblets; reserve for other uses or discard. Rinse the chicken inside and out; pat dry. Spoon the seasoning mixture into the body cavity. Close the cavity with a small skewer. Place the chicken in a bowl; cover and refrigerate overnight.

Preheat the oven to 450°. Line a roasting pan with a sheet of foil large enough to wrap around sides of the chicken. Place a layer of salt in the center of the foil. Place the chicken, breast side up, on the salt. Pat the salt all over the top and sides of the chicken. Sprinkle the water over the salt so it forms a casing. Bake, uncovered, for 1 hour.

Transfer the chicken and foil to a cutting board and let stand for 10 minutes. Scrape off the salt; discard the foil and salt. If any salt spills on the cutting board, wipe the board clean before slicing the meat. Cut the chicken into serving-size pieces and arrange on a serving platter. Serve hot or cold.

CHICKEN WITH FIVE-SPICED SALT

There's more to poaching than boiling water. But don't worry, if you can boil water and follow my easy instructions, you will have poached chicken that is beyond reproach.

Makes 4 to 6 servings

1 WHOLE FRYING CHICKEN (3 TO
   4 POUNDS)
SESAME OIL

Seasonings

5 SLICES GINGER, LIGHTLY CRUSHED
3 GREEN ONIONS, CUT IN HALF AND
   LIGHTLY CRUSHED
1 STAR ANISE

Five-Spiced Salt

2 TEASPOONS GARLIC SALT
$\frac{1}{2}$ TEASPOON GROUND SICHUAN
   PEPPERCORNS
$\frac{1}{4}$ TEASPOON CHINESE FIVE-SPICE
   POWDER
$\frac{1}{4}$ TEASPOON CAYENNE PEPPER

Remove the chicken neck and giblets; reserve for other uses or discard. Rinse the chicken inside and out; pat dry.

Place the chicken, breast side up, in a large pot. Add the seasonings and enough water to cover the chicken. Bring to a boil over high heat. Reduce the heat to low, cover, and simmer for 20 to 25 minutes. Turn off the heat and let stand until the meat is no longer pink when cut near thighbone, about 30 minutes longer.

Remove the chicken from the pot and rub with the sesame oil. Reserve the poaching liquid for another use.

Combine the five-spiced salt ingredients in a frying pan. Cook, stirring, over low heat until toasted and fragrant, 2 to 3 minutes. Let cool.

Cut the chicken into 2-inch pieces or carve, Western-style; arrange on a serving platter. Serve with the five-spiced salt on the side for dipping.

Worth One's Salt

When is a dipping sauce not a sauce? When it's five-spiced salt! While soy sauce is the most common sauce for cooking and dipping, it takes a backseat to a spicy salt in adding a unique and exciting taste to this chicken dish. This combination of cayenne pepper, Chinese five-spice powder, garlic salt, and ground Sichuan peppercorn is a true tour de force.

FIERY SICHUAN CHICKEN

To those of us who are spice fans, Sichuan cuisine is fondly referred to as a trial by fire—fiery hot, that is, as in this chicken recipe. When you add chile garlic sauce to dried red chiles and toasted peppercorns, the result is pure TNT.

Makes 4 servings

½ TEASPOON SICHUAN PEPPERCORNS
12 OUNCES BONELESS, SKINLESS
    CHICKEN BREASTS, CUT INTO
    ¾-INCH PIECES
2 TABLESPOONS OYSTER SAUCE

Sauce

¼ CUP CHICKEN STOCK
1 TABLESPOON SOY SAUCE
1 TEASPOON SESAME OIL
1 TEASPOON CHILE GARLIC SAUCE
1 TEASPOON SUGAR
½ TEASPOON CORNSTARCH

• • •

2 TABLESPOONS COOKING OIL
6 SMALL DRIED RED CHILES
2 TABLESPOONS CHOPPED SICHUAN
    PRESERVED VEGETABLE
2 TEASPOONS FINELY CHOPPED GARLIC
SLICED GREEN ONION

Place the peppercorns in a small frying pan over medium heat. Cook, shaking the pan frequently, until the peppercorns darken slightly and smell toasted, 3 to 4 minutes. Process in a spice grinder or blender until coarsely ground.

Place the chicken in a bowl and add the oyster sauce; stir to coat. Let stand for 15 minutes. Combine the sauce ingredients in a bowl.

Place a wok or wide frying pan over high heat until hot. Add the oil, swirling to coat the sides. Add the chiles and cook, stirring, until fragrant, about 5 seconds. Add the chicken and stir-fry for 2 minutes. Add the preserved vegetable, garlic, and peppercorns; stir-fry for 1 minute. Add the sauce and cook, stirring, until it boils and thickens. Place on a serving platter and garnish with the green onion.

The Wild Wild West
Our spice scale goes up the farther west we travel in China. The climate in Sichuan province is hot and humid, and the food is well known for its explosive combination of hot, sour, sweet, and salty tastes. Spices rule here: Sichuan peppercorns, star anise, and hot chiles, the prince of Sichuan spice.

SHAO HSING WINE CHICKEN

A drink before dinner? How about one in your dinner? Here is the classic chilled chicken dish from Shanghai—let it be the toast of your next dinner party. Cheers!

Makes 4 to 6 servings

1 WHOLE FRYING CHICKEN
   (3 TO 3½ POUNDS)
6 SLICES GINGER, LIGHTLY CRUSHED

Wine Sauce

1 CUP SHAO HSING WINE
⅓ CUP CHICKEN STOCK
¼ CUP SOY SAUCE
2 TEASPOONS FINELY CHOPPED GINGER
2 TEASPOONS SUGAR
1 TEASPOON SESAME OIL
¼ TEASPOON WHITE PEPPER

Remove the chicken neck and giblets; reserve for other uses or discard. Rinse the chicken inside and out; pat dry. Place the chicken, breast side up, in a pot. Add the ginger and enough water to cover the chicken. Bring to a boil over high heat. Reduce the heat to low; cover and simmer until the meat is no longer pink when cut near the thighbone, about 40 minutes. Remove the chicken from the pot and let it cool to room temperature.

If desired, remove and discard the skin from the chicken. Cut the meat into bite-size pieces or shred it; place in a bowl.

Combine the sauce ingredients in a pan. Cook over medium heat until heated through. Do not boil. Pour the sauce over the chicken and stir to coat. Cover and refrigerate overnight. Serve cold.

Ask, and Thou Shao Receive

Shao Hsing wine is a brew of fermented rice wine that is putting Zhejiang province of eastern China on every gourmet's wine map. Local lake water and fermented rice are poured into huge urns, then a century-old strain of yeast is added and the urn is covered with mats made from seaweed. The brewing process can take from 18 months all the way up to a hundred years.

SOY SAUCE CHICKEN

This is a popular dish in Chinese delis all over the world. Look closely and you will find soy sauce chickens hanging in the window next to barbecued roast pork and spareribs. But it's really easy to create the chickens at home. Just follow this recipe and turn your kitchen into your neighborhood's newest Chinese deli.

Makes 4 to 6 servings

1 WHOLE FRYING CHICKEN (3 TO
   3½ POUNDS)
4 SLICES GINGER, LIGHTLY CRUSHED
4 GREEN ONIONS, LIGHTLY CRUSHED
   AND CUT IN HALF

Sauce

3 CUPS CHICKEN STOCK OR WATER
1½ CUPS DARK SOY SAUCE
1 CUP CHINESE RICE WINE OR DRY
   SHERRY
⅔ CUP LIGHT SOY SAUCE
⅓ CUP ROCK SUGAR OR
   ¼ CUP SUGAR
3 STAR ANISE
3 CINNAMON STICKS

Remove the chicken neck and giblets; reserve for other uses or discard. Rinse the chicken inside and out; pat dry. Place the ginger and green onions inside the body cavity; air-dry for 30 minutes.

Combine the sauce ingredients in a pot. Bring to a boil over medium-high heat. Add the chicken, breast side down. Cover and bring to a boil. Reduce the heat to low; cover and simmer for 40 minutes. Turn off the heat and let stand, covered, for 20 minutes.

Cut the chicken into serving-size pieces and arrange on a serving platter. Spoon the sauce over the chicken. Serve hot, or cover and refrigerate and serve cold.

Soy What?

Not all soy sauces look or taste alike. Regular light soy is used to give Chinese dishes their characteristic flavor and light brown color. Dark soy, which is soy sauce with molasses added, is thicker, sweeter, and (of course) darker. It is more commonly used in braising dishes. Reflecting current food and health trends, reduced-sodium soy sauce is now a very popular item on grocery shelves. It contains about 40 percent less sodium than regular soy sauce, but it's just as flavorful.

TANGY CITRUS CHICKEN

Many of my friends in Europe and North America had their first taste of Chinese food in a plate of sweet and sour chicken. I call it the pioneer of Chinese cooking in the West. Over the years, these "pioneers" have all settled, grown roots, and evolved with new ingredients and new tastes. For an updated version, try this Tangy Citrus Chicken.

Makes 4 servings

4 BONELESS, SKINLESS CHICKEN
   BREASTS

Marinade

1 TABLESPOON CHINESE RICE WINE OR
   DRY SHERRY
1/4 TEASPOON SALT

Sauce

1 CUP SWEET AND SOUR SAUCE
1/4 CUP FRESHLY SQUEEZED
   LEMON JUICE
1 TABLESPOON GRATED LEMON ZEST

1 CUP ALL-PURPOSE FLOUR
1/4 CUP SESAME SEEDS
1 EGG, LIGHTLY BEATEN
CORNSTARCH
4 TABLESPOONS COOKING OIL
LEMON SLICES

Place the chicken pieces between 2 sheets of plastic wrap and pound lightly with the flat side of a mallet until about 1/4 inch thick. Combine the marinade ingredients in a bowl. Add the chicken and turn to coat. Let stand for 15 minutes. Combine the sauce ingredients in a pan.

Combine the flour and sesame seeds in a bowl. Dredge the chicken pieces in the flour mixture; shake to remove the excess. Dip in egg, drain briefly, and coat with cornstarch.

Place a wide nonstick frying pan over medium heat. Add 2 tablespoons of the oil, swirling to coat the sides. Place half the chicken in the pan; cook, turning once, until golden brown and the meat is no longer pink when cut, 6 to 8 minutes. Remove from the pan and cover loosely with foil. Heat the remaining oil and cook the remaining chicken pieces.

Place the sauce over medium heat and cook, stirring, until the sauce boils.

To serve, cut the chicken crosswise into slices about 1 inch wide, then reassemble in its original shape on a serving platter. Pour the sauce over the chicken and garnish with the lemon slices.

Zest Appeal

The most fragrant part of a citrus fruit lies in its outer peel. This is where the fragrant oil is lodged. Use a zester to extract zests. Use only the yellow outer peel and not the bitter white part underneath.

HONEY-GLAZED CHICKEN WITH LYCHEE FRUIT

In my mind, the sweetest lychees were always from my neighbor's garden in China. As children, we used to crane our necks and raise our eyes every summer night toward those trees, waiting for the first sign of a ripe lychee on the branch. Thanks to modern technology, lychees are now available in the West both fresh and in cans. Great news for those of you whose neighbor doesn't have a lychee tree around the house.

Makes 4 servings

Marinade

2 TABLESPOONS LIGHT SOY SAUCE

2 TEASPOONS CORNSTARCH

• • •

12 OUNCES BONELESS, SKINLESS
    CHICKEN BREASTS, CUT INTO
    3/4-INCH PIECES

Sauce

1/4 CUP CHICKEN STOCK

3 TABLESPOONS HONEY

2 TABLESPOONS FRESHLY SQUEEZED
    LEMON JUICE

2 TEASPOONS LIGHT SOY SAUCE

1 TEASPOON DARK SOY SAUCE

1 TEASPOON CORNSTARCH

• • •

2 TABLESPOONS COOKING OIL

15 OUNCES LYCHEES

Combine the marinade ingredients in a bowl. Add the chicken and stir to coat. Let stand for 15 minutes. Combine the sauce ingredients in a bowl.

Place a wok or wide frying pan over high heat until hot. Add the oil, swirling to coat the sides. Add the chicken and stir-fry for 2 minutes. Add the sauce and cook, stirring, until the sauce boils and thickens. Add the lychees and cook until heated through. Place on a serving platter and serve.

Lychee Internationale

The delicate lychee fruit has gone international! Once found mainly in Southern China, lychees are now planted in the United States. Florida and Hawaii, for example, grow them from July to September. So if you find yourself in the Sunshine or Aloha States during the summer months, keep an eye out for the fresh fruits.

SPICED CORNISH GAME HENS WITH SIZZLING OIL

The Chinese dining table is game for just about any fowl. This recipe is adapted from a classical banquet dish of roast pigeons. The flavorful sizzling oil adds an unusual finishing touch.

Makes 4 servings

Dry Rub

2 TEASPOONS SICHUAN PEPPERCORNS

2 TEASPOONS FINELY CHOPPED GARLIC

2 TEASPOONS FINELY CHOPPED GINGER

. . .

2 CORNISH GAME HENS

4 SLICES GINGER, LIGHTLY CRUSHED

2 GREEN ONIONS, CUT INTO
  2-INCH PIECES

1 TABLESPOON COOKING OIL

Sizzling Oil

3 SLICES GINGER, JULIENNED

1 GREEN ONION, JULIENNED

3 TABLESPOONS COOKING OIL

3 TABLESPOONS SOY SAUCE

Place the peppercorns in a small frying pan over medium heat. Cook, shaking pan frequently, until the peppercorns darken slightly and smell toasted, 3 to 4 minutes. Process in a spice grinder or blender until coarsely ground. In a bowl, combine the ground peppercorns, garlic, and ginger.

Remove the necks and giblets from the birds; reserve for other uses or discard. Rinse the birds inside and out; pat dry. Rub inside and out with the dry rub. Cover and refrigerate for 1 to 2 hours.

Preheat the oven to 350°. Place the birds, breast side down, on a rack in a foil-lined shallow roasting pan. Place half the ginger and green onion inside the body cavity of each bird, then tuck wings under. Roast for 30 minutes. Turn the birds over, brush with the oil, and continue to roast until the meat is no longer pink when cut near the thighbone, 30 to 45 minutes longer, depending on the size of the birds. Remove from the oven. Cover loosely with foil and let stand for 10 minutes.

Prepare the sizzling oil: Place the ginger and green onion in a heatproof bowl. Heat the oil in a pan over high heat until smoking. Pour the oil over the ginger and onion. Add the soy sauce.

To serve, cut each bird in half. Pour some of the sizzling oil over each.

STEAMED CHICKEN WINGS WITH MUSHROOMS AND LOP CHEONG

The wonderful aroma of freshly steamed lop cheong *(Chinese pork sausage) always reminds me of rushing home from school for lunch. For an extra treat, my mother would steam them with chicken and black mushrooms, and this is still one of my favorite family recipes.*

Makes 6 servings

8 DRIED BLACK (SHIITAKE) MUSHROOMS

2 DRIED WOOD EAR MUSHROOMS (OPTIONAL)

1¾ POUNDS CHICKEN WINGS OR THIGHS

4 OUNCES CHINESE SAUSAGES *(LOP CHEONG)*, CUT DIAGONALLY INTO ½-INCH SLICES

5 SLICES GINGER, LIGHTLY CRUSHED AND CUT IN HALF

3 TABLESPOONS SLICED SICHUAN PRESERVED VEGETABLE

1 GREEN ONION, SLICED

1 TABLESPOON CHINESE RICE WINE OR DRY SHERRY

1 TEASPOON SALT

Soak the 2 kinds of mushrooms separately in warm water to cover until softened, about 15 minutes; drain. Discard the black mushroom stems and cut the caps in half. Cut the wood ears into bite-size pieces.

Separate the chicken wings into sections; reserve the bony tips for other uses or discard. If using chicken thighs, bone if desired. Place the chicken in a pot and cover with water; bring to a boil. Parboil for 1 minute; drain. Place the chicken in a 2-quart casserole and add the remaining ingredients; cover.

Place a steamer basket or metal steamer rack in a wok, and pour boiling water up to a point just below the steaming rack. Place the covered casserole on the rack; cover and steam over high heat until the chicken is tender, 1½ to 2 hours. Add more boiling water to the steamer as needed.

Take Wing

In the West, the breast is most often the preferred part of the chicken. In French cuisine, the chicken breast is referred to as a *suprême*. To be shown honor and respect in China, however, a guest is offered a chicken drumstick, thigh, or wing. So next time you're offered a drumstick at a Chinese dinner, smile graciously; you are being honored.

PEKING DUCK AT HOME

Anyone who visits Beijing should not miss trying the world-famous Peking Duck. In some restaurants you have to order this 24 hours in advance. Why bother? You can follow this recipe and do it at home.

Makes 4 to 6 servings

1 WHOLE DUCK (4 TO 5 POUNDS), CLEANED
2 CLOVES GARLIC, LIGHTLY CRUSHED
2 SLICES GINGER, LIGHTLY CRUSHED
2 GREEN ONIONS, LIGHTLY CRUSHED

Marinade

3 TABLESPOONS SOY SAUCE
2 TEASPOONS FINELY CHOPPED GARLIC
2 TEASPOONS FINELY CHOPPED GINGER

Basting Liquid

3 TABLESPOONS SOY SAUCE
2 TABLESPOONS CHINESE RICE WINE OR DRY SHERRY
2 TABLESPOONS HOISIN SAUCE
1/2 TEASPOON CHINESE FIVE-SPICE POWDER
1/2 TEASPOON WHITE PEPPER

Glaze

3 TABLESPOONS HONEY
3 TABLESPOONS RICE VINEGAR
2 TABLESPOONS SOY SAUCE

Discard the excess fat from the neck and body cavity of the duck. Bring a large pot of water to a boil. Add the duck and parboil for 3 minutes; drain. Let cool slightly, then pat dry with paper towels. Insert the crushed garlic, ginger, and green onions under the duck skin.

Combine the marinade ingredients in a small bowl. Pour the marinade into the duck cavity. Cover the duck and refrigerate for 2 to 4 hours.

Combine the basting liquid ingredients in a bowl. Combine the glaze ingredients in a pan. Cook, stirring, over medium heat, until heated through.

Preheat the oven to 350°. Place the duck, breast side down, on a rack in a foil-lined roasting pan. Roast for 30 minutes. Turn the duck, breast side up, and roast, brushing occasionally with the basting liquid, for 30 minutes. Increase the heat to 400° and continue to roast until the skin is browned and crisp and the meat is no longer pink when cut near the thighbone, about 20 minutes. Brush the duck with the glaze. Let stand for 10 minutes.

Drain the juices from the cavity into a pan. Transfer the duck to a cutting board and cut the meat and skin into thin slices; arrange on a serving platter. Skim the fat from the juices; reheat the juices and pour over the duck just before serving.

Skin-deep Beauty?

The famous Peking Duck and the Cantonese Roast Duck are well known for their crisp, golden brown skin. To get a nice crispy skin, you first blanch the duck in boiling water, then rub it with a tangy mixture of honey, vinegar, and ginger. Then hang the duck up (preferably overnight) so the skin becomes taut and dry before roasting.

RED-COOKED DUCK

Here is a perfectly good way to serve up a tender, golden brown duck without baking it. Try this recipe, and you can send your oven on a holiday.

Makes 6 to 8 servings

Marinade

2 TABLESPOONS DARK SOY SAUCE

1 TABLESPOON CHINESE RICE WINE OR
   DRY SHERRY

• • •

1 WHOLE DUCK (4 TO 5 POUNDS)

Sauce

1½ QUARTS CHICKEN STOCK

½ CUP CHINESE RICE WINE OR DRY
   SHERRY

½ CUP DARK SOY SAUCE

8 SLICES GINGER, LIGHTLY CRUSHED

6 CLOVES GARLIC, FINELY CHOPPED

4 GREEN ONIONS, CUT IN HALF

4 STAR ANISE

2 CINNAMON STICKS

3 TABLESPOONS SUGAR

2 TEASPOONS SESAME OIL

• • •

2 TABLESPOONS COOKING OIL

8 OUNCES NAPA CABBAGE, LEAVES
   SEPARATED AND CUT INTO
   BITE-SIZE PIECES

1½ TEASPOONS CORNSTARCH DISSOLVED
   IN 1 TABLESPOON WATER

CUCUMBER SLICES

Combine the marinade ingredients in a bowl.

Discard the excess fat from the neck and body cavity of the duck. Rinse the duck inside and out; pat dry. Prick all over with a skewer. Rub the duck inside and out with the marinade. Cover and refrigerate for 1 hour. Drain the duck.

Combine the sauce ingredients in a pot.

Place a wok or wide frying pan over medium-high heat until hot. Add the oil, swirling to coat the sides. Add the duck and cook until evenly browned all over, about 10 minutes.

Bring the sauce to a boil over medium heat. Add the duck; reduce the heat to low, cover, and simmer, turning occasionally, until the duck is tender and the skin is a rich brown, about 1 hour.

Bring a pan of water to a boil. Add the cabbage; cook until tender-crisp, 2 to 3 minutes. Drain well.

Carefully lift the duck from the pot, reserving the sauce. Bone the duck, if desired, then cut into serving-size pieces. Place the duck pieces on a heatproof serving platter, arranging them in the shape of a whole duck. Keep warm in a 200° oven.

Skim and discard the fat from the braising sauce. Place ½ cup of the braising sauce in a pan. Bring to a boil over medium heat. Add the cornstarch mixture and cook, stirring, until the sauce boils and thickens.

Arrange the cabbage around the duck. Pour the sauce over the duck and garnish with the cucumber slices.

Seeing Red

Red cooking is a popular Chinese method of slow cooking. The meats are browned in a pan or a wok, then simmered slowly in a rich sauce made from soy sauce and sugar. The meat will take on a reddish brown glaze, a juicy and tender texture, and a rich, full-bodied taste. In many Chinese restaurants, the sauce is saved and used over and over as a master sauce.

PINEAPPLE GINGER DUCK

The sweet taste of fruit goes so well with duck that you can find this combination in many cuisines. One of the best known and most popular is the French Duck à l'Orange.

Makes 4 to 6 servings

Seasonings

2 TABLESPOONS CHICKEN STOCK

1 TABLESPOON PLUM SAUCE

1 TABLESPOON CHINESE RICE WINE OR
   DRY SHERRY

1 TEASPOON CORNSTARCH

* * *

2 TABLESPOONS COOKING OIL

2 GREEN ONIONS, CUT INTO
   1-INCH PIECES

10 MINT LEAVES

1/2 RED BELL PEPPER, SEEDED AND CUT
   INTO DIAMONDS

1 CUP PINEAPPLE CHUNKS

1/4 CUP SWEET PICKLED GINGER, CUT
   INTO DIAMONDS

4 CHINESE ROAST DUCK BREASTS,
   THINLY SLICED

Combine the seasoning ingredients in a bowl.

Place a wok or wide frying pan over high heat until hot. Add the oil, swirling to coat the sides. Add the green onions and mint; cook, stirring, until fragrant, about 30 seconds. Add the bell pepper, pineapple, and ginger; stir-fry for 30 seconds. Add the duck and seasonings; cook, stirring, until heated through.

By Western standards, the Chinese diet is light on meat and heavy on grain and vegetables. When meat is served, it is used more as a flavoring agent than as the main part of the dish. Geography and economics are two determining factors. In most of China, high population density limits the space available for cattle ranching. It is therefore not surprising that the most popular meat is pork, since pigs can live on household scraps. In fact, the Chinese character for the word "meat" mostly refers to pork. For beef, a preceding character of cow is added, making the word's literal meaning "cow meat."

As the Chinese diet becomes more international, beef now plays a more visible role, in home kitchens as well as on restaurant menus. For this chapter, I have selected several of my favorite beef dishes. Note that the Chinese taste goes beyond filet mignon, T-bone, London broil, and porterhouse; oxtail, beef liver, and even beef tongue are all fair game in my kitchen.

I have also included a couple of recipes for lamb. Mutton is popular in China's northwestern provinces. Many Southern Chinese find the taste of lamb a bit too strong, so to them I suggest the slow braising method of "red cooking."

Sichuan Beef with Citrus Peel

This is a classic dish from Sichuan province. It also happens to be my family's favorite. It is quick and delicious.

Makes 4 servings

3 PIECES DRIED TANGERINE PEEL

Marinade

1½ TABLESPOONS DARK SOY SAUCE

1 TABLESPOON CORNSTARCH

• • •

12 OUNCES FLANK STEAK, THINLY
    SLICED DIAGONALLY

Sauce

3 TABLESPOONS FROZEN ORANGE JUICE
    CONCENTRATE, THAWED

1 TABLESPOON LIGHT SOY SAUCE

1 TABLESPOON SUGAR

1½ TEASPOONS CORNSTARCH

1 TEASPOON CHILE GARLIC SAUCE

• • •

2 TABLESPOONS COOKING OIL

4 SMALL DRIED RED CHILES

4 GREEN ONIONS, CUT DIAGONALLY INTO
    2-INCH LENGTHS

ORANGE SEGMENTS

Soak the tangerine peel in warm water to cover until softened, about 15 minutes. Reserve the tangerine peel soaking liquid. Scrape and discard the white pith from the back of the peel. Cut the peel into thin strips.

In a bowl, combine the marinade ingredients and 2 tablespoons of the reserved tangerine peel soaking liquid. Add the beef and stir to coat. Let stand for 30 minutes. Combine the sauce ingredients in a bowl.

Place a wok or wide frying pan over high heat until hot. Add 1 tablespoon of the oil, swirling to coat the sides. Add the chiles and cook, stirring, until fragrant, about 10 seconds. Add the beef and stir-fry until barely pink, about 2 minutes. Remove the beef and chiles from the wok.

Add the remaining oil to the wok, swirling to coat the sides. Add the tangerine peel and stir-fry for 1 minute. Add the green onions and stir-fry for 1 minute. Add the sauce and cook, stirring, until the sauce boils and thickens. Return the beef and chiles to the wok; mix well. Place on a serving platter and garnish with the orange segments.

Tangible Tangerine

Around Chinese New Year, tangerines are in season, and I remember my mother used to save the tangerine peels for our kitchen. You can do the same: Peel the fruit and cut the peel into pieces, scraping away the white pith from the inside. Dry the peels in the open air (sun-drying is best) until they are firm and somewhat brittle, then store them in an airtight jar.

BEEF IN OYSTER SAUCE WITH BROCCOLI

This dish is the ultimate standby in many Chinese restaurants and can be in your kitchen as well. It is simple, delicious, ready in minutes, and always satisfying. What more can we ask of any dish?

Makes 2 to 4 servings

Marinade

1 TABLESPOON LIGHT SOY SAUCE

1½ TEASPOONS CHINESE RICE WINE OR
    DRY SHERRY

1 TEASPOON CORNSTARCH

. . .

8 OUNCES FLANK STEAK, THINLY SLICED
    DIAGONALLY

Sauce

¾ CUP CHICKEN STOCK

1 TABLESPOON OYSTER SAUCE

2 TEASPOONS DARK SOY SAUCE

1 TEASPOON SUGAR

. . .

2 TABLESPOONS COOKING OIL

2 TEASPOONS FINELY CHOPPED GARLIC

6 OUNCES BROCCOLI FLORETS

2 OUNCES FRESH SHIITAKE
    MUSHROOMS, STEMS DISCARDED AND
    CUT IN HALF

1 TEASPOON CORNSTARCH DISSOLVED IN
    2 TEASPOONS WATER

Combine the marinade ingredients in a bowl. Add the beef and stir to coat. Let stand for 30 minutes. Combine the sauce ingredients in a bowl.

Place a wok or wide frying pan over high heat until hot. Add the oil, swirling to coat the sides. Add the garlic and cook, stirring, until fragrant, about 10 seconds. Add the beef and stir-fry until barely pink, about 1½ minutes. Remove the beef from the wok.

Add the broccoli and mushrooms; stir-fry for 30 seconds. Add the sauce and bring to a boil. Reduce the heat to medium-high and cook until the broccoli is tender-crisp, about 3 minutes. Add the cornstarch mixture and cook, stirring, until the sauce boils and thickens. Return the beef to the wok and mix well.

Brokering Broccoli

I grew up with Chinese broccoli (*gai lan*), which has thin, dark green stems and leaves, and many tiny white flowers. When cooked, the stems become tender and they have a pleasantly bittersweet taste. In recent years, Western broccoli has made inroads in Asia, and now it is not unusual to find it in restaurant dishes in Shanghai, Taipei, and Hong Kong. At the same time, Chinese broccoli is appearing in more and more markets in the West.

SPICY GINGER BEEF

In Chinese cooking, we often combine fresh and preserved forms of the same ingredient in the same dish. Adding pickled ginger to fresh ginger gives this beef dish a sophisticated and complex taste.

Makes 2 to 4 servings

Marinade

1 TABLESPOON DARK SOY SAUCE
2 TEASPOONS CORNSTARCH
1½ TEASPOONS COOKING OIL

◆ ◆ ◆

8 OUNCES FLANK STEAK, THINLY SLICED
    DIAGONALLY

Seasonings

1 TABLESPOON LIGHT SOY SAUCE
2 TEASPOONS SESAME OIL

◆ ◆ ◆

1½ TABLESPOONS COOKING OIL
¼ CUP GINGER, JULIENNED
½ GREEN BELL PEPPER, SEEDED AND
    THINLY SLICED
½ RED BELL PEPPER, SEEDED AND
    THINLY SLICED
¼ CUP SWEET PICKLED GINGER,
    JULIENNED

Combine the marinade ingredients in a bowl. Add the beef and stir to coat. Let stand for 30 minutes. Combine the seasoning ingredients in a bowl.

Place a wok or wide frying pan over high heat until hot. Add 1 tablespoon of the oil, swirling to coat the sides. Add the beef and stir-fry until barely pink, about 1½ minutes. Remove the beef from the wok.

Add the remaining oil to the wok, swirling to coat the sides. Add the ginger and bell peppers; stir-fry until the peppers are tender-crisp, about 1 minute. Add the seasonings and pickled ginger; cook until heated through. Return the beef to the wok and mix well.

The Many Faces of Ginger

Fresh ginger has smooth, pale golden skin and a spicy, aromatic interior. Young ginger is slightly pink and has a delicate (some might say sweeter) flavor. Crystallized ginger is young ginger cooked in sugar syrup and coated in sugar. Pickled ginger is cured in brine, then soaked in a sugar-vinegar mixture. Preserved ginger is packed in a heavy sugar syrup. So, next time don't just say ginger, say "which ginger?"

BRAISED BEEF SHANK

In the mood for a dish with a bold and robust taste? Try this spiced beef shank and let the combination of fennel, star anise, cinnamon, and soy take your taste buds for an incredible ride.

Makes 6 to 8 servings

1½ TO 2 POUNDS BEEF SHANK

Seasonings

2½ CUPS WATER

2 CUPS CHICKEN STOCK

3 TABLESPOONS ROCK SUGAR

2 TABLESPOONS LIGHT SOY SAUCE

4 STAR ANISE

2 CINNAMON STICKS

1 TEASPOON FENNEL SEEDS

Sauce

¼ CUP SEASONED RICE VINEGAR

3 GREEN ONIONS, CHOPPED

2 TABLESPOONS CHOPPED GARLIC

2 TABLESPOONS DARK SOY SAUCE

1½ TABLESPOONS SESAME OIL

½ TEASPOON CHILE GARLIC SAUCE

Place the shank and the seasoning ingredients in a medium pan. Bring to a boil. Cover and simmer over low heat for 2 to 2½ hours. Let cool. Cover and refrigerate overnight.

Combine the sauce ingredients in a pan. Cook, stirring, over medium heat until heated through. Place in a small serving bowl.

Remove the shank from the pan and thinly slice the meat. Arrange the meat on a serving platter and serve with the sauce on the side.

Pressure for Pleasure

In today's rush-rush-go-go lifestyle, a pressure cooker can be a good friend in the kitchen. To make Braised Beef Shank in this way, simply mix all the seasoning ingredients with the beef in a pressure cooker. Cover and cook according to manufacturer's instructions, about 30 minutes. Quite a change from hours at the stove! When you are ready, so shall your dinner be.

CHINESE LAMB STEW

The arid high plains in Northwest China are much better suited for herding sheep than planting crops, so understandably, lamb is a major source of meat protein in the local diet. This recipe brings a touch of the Northwest by way of "red cooking," which was first popularized in the coastal city of Shanghai. Who says Chinese cooking is not a melting pot?

Makes 4 to 6 servings

1 PIECE DRIED TANGERINE PEEL

Sauce

1 QUART CHICKEN STOCK

⅓ CUP DARK SOY SAUCE

¼ CUP LIGHT SOY SAUCE

¼ CUP CHINESE RICE WINE OR DRY SHERRY

2 TABLESPOONS SUGAR

* * *

2 TABLESPOONS COOKING OIL

6 SLICES GINGER, LIGHTLY CRUSHED

4 CLOVES GARLIC, CRUSHED

1 TEASPOON CHINESE FIVE-SPICE POWDER

3 POUNDS LAMB SHOULDER OR LEG

¾ CUP CHICKEN STOCK

9 OUNCES DAIKON, CUT INTO 1-INCH CUBES

1 SMALL CARROT, DICED

2 TEASPOONS CORNSTARCH DISSOLVED IN 2 TEASPOONS WATER

Age for Beauty

Many Chinese restaurants save their red-cooked sauce to use as a base or master sauce in other recipes. After each use, the chef adds in a little stock, a dash of soy sauce, and more seasonings. With each use, the sauce gets richer in taste and the flavor of the meat is retained. In judging a master sauce, it is always age before beauty.

Soak the tangerine peel in warm water to cover until softened, about 15 minutes. Reserve the tangerine peel soaking liquid. Scrape and discard the white pith from the back of the peel. Cut the peel into thin strips. Combine the sauce ingredients in a bowl.

Place a pan over high heat until hot. Add the oil, swirling to coat the sides. Add the ginger and garlic; cook, stirring, until fragrant, about 10 seconds. Add the tangerine peel and sauce; bring to a boil. Reduce the heat to low, cover, and simmer for 20 minutes. Add the five-spice powder; mix well.

Meanwhile, place the lamb in a pot just large enough to hold it snugly; add enough water to cover the lamb. Bring to a boil over high heat. Cook for 4 minutes and drain. Remove the lamb and rinse the pot.

Return the lamb to the pot and add the sauce. Add the reserved tangerine peel soaking liquid and enough water to cover the lamb. Bring to a boil over high heat. Reduce the heat to low; cover and simmer until the lamb is tender when pierced, about 40 minutes.

Remove the lamb from the pot. Let stand for 10 minutes. Strain the sauce through a fine sieve into a bowl. Place ½ cup of the sauce in a pan. Add the stock, daikon, and carrot. Bring to a boil over medium-high heat. Add the cornstarch mixture and cook, stirring, until the sauce boils and thickens.

Remove the lamb from the pot and thinly slice. Arrange the sliced lamb on a serving platter and serve with the sauce on the side.

MINT-FLAVORED SKEWERED MEAT

Chunks of meat on skewers are popular Middle Eastern treats, but they are just as popular in Northwestern China. Some of my best memories of meat on skewers came from a street stand in the ancient city of Xian. For a more contemporary taste in this dish, I add a touch of mint.

Makes 4 servings

12 OUNCES BONELESS LAMB (LEG OR
    LOIN) OR BEEF

Marinade

1 TEASPOON SICHUAN PEPPERCORNS
1/3 CUP CHINESE RICE WINE OR DRY
    SHERRY
1/4 CUP SOY SAUCE
2 TABLESPOONS CHOPPED MINT
2 TEASPOONS FINELY CHOPPED GARLIC
2 TEASPOONS CORNSTARCH

ABOUT 16 BAMBOO SKEWERS
2 TABLESPOONS COOKING OIL
1/2 TEASPOON FINELY CHOPPED GARLIC
1/2 TEASPOON FINELY CHOPPED GINGER
1 ZUCCHINI, SLICED
1 ONION, SLICED
1/2 GREEN BELL PEPPER, SEEDED AND
    SLICED
1/2 RED BELL PEPPER, SEEDED AND
    SLICED

Grill for Thrill

In most parts of China, grilling is not a common method of cooking, but in the open-air food court of Xian, life is simply a grill a minute. The city's open-air eating emporium claims to be the largest one of its kind in the world. On an average night, 20,000 customers are served. I suppose the local definition of eating out is to have your meals at these open-air eateries.

Cut the meat into thin strips, about 1/2 inch wide and 8 inches long.

Place the peppercorns in a small frying pan over medium heat. Cook, shaking the pan frequently, until the peppercorns darken slightly and smell toasted, 3 to 4 minutes. Process in a blender or spice grinder until coarsely ground. In a bowl, combine peppercorns with other marinade ingredients. Add the meat and stir to coat. Let stand for 30 minutes. Soak the skewers in warm water to cover for 15 minutes; drain.

Remove the meat from the marinade; reserve the marinade. Thread one piece of meat on each skewer, stretching the meat so it lies flat.

To cook, place the skewers on a greased grill 3 to 4 inches above a solid bed of glowing coals. Cook, basting with the reserved marinade, until the meat is barely pink, about 1 minute on each side.

Place the remaining marinade in a pan. Bring to a boil over medium-high heat. Pour into a small serving bowl.

Place a wok or wide frying pan over high heat until hot. Add the oil, swirling to coat the sides. Add the garlic and ginger; cook, stirring, until fragrant, about 10 seconds. Add the zucchini, onion, and bell peppers; stir-fry until the onion is tender-crisp, 2 to 4 minutes.

Spread the vegetable mixture on a serving platter. Place the skewered meat on top and serve with the sauce on the side.

THE GREAT KHAN'S FIRE POT

Did the Swiss invent fondue? Not according to the Mongolian warriors. The greatest culinary contribution of the Great Khan was undoubtedly the Mongolian fire pot, which metamorphosed in the West into a fondue pot. But instead of cheese, the fire pot cooks meat and other ingredients in a savory broth. The Mongol emperors must have thrown some lively dinner parties.

Makes 6 to 8 servings

3 OUNCES DRIED BEAN THREAD
  NOODLES

12 OUNCES SPINACH, WASHED AND
  TOUGH STEMS DISCARDED

2 POUNDS BONELESS LAMB (LEG OR
  LOIN), CHICKEN, OR BEEF, CUT INTO
  THIN STRIPS

1 POUND MEDIUM RAW SHRIMP,
  SHELLED AND DEVEINED (OPTIONAL)

2 GREEN ONIONS, CUT INTO 1-INCH
  LENGTHS

* * *

2 QUARTS CHICKEN STOCK

1 SLICE GINGER, LIGHTLY CRUSHED

2 TABLESPOONS CHINESE RICE WINE OR
  DRY SHERRY

Dipping Sauces

1: *Hot and Spicy Sauce*

¼ CUP CHICKEN STOCK

2 TABLESPOONS SOY SAUCE

1 TABLESPOON SESAME OIL

1 TABLESPOON FINELY CHOPPED GARLIC

1 TABLESPOON FINELY CHOPPED GINGER

1 TEASPOON CHILE GARLIC SAUCE

1 TEASPOON CHOPPED CILANTRO

2: *Spicy Hoisin Paste*

3 TABLESPOONS HOISIN SAUCE

2 TABLESPOONS CHICKEN STOCK

1 TABLESPOON SOY SAUCE

1 TEASPOON CHILE GARLIC SAUCE

1 TEASPOON SESAME OIL

1 TEASPOON WORCESTERSHIRE SAUCE

3: *Tangy Mustard Sauce*

3 TABLESPOONS CHICKEN STOCK

3 TABLESPOONS PREPARED CHINESE
  MUSTARD

2 TABLESPOONS SESAME OIL

1 TABLESPOON FINELY CHOPPED GARLIC

1 TABLESPOON FINELY CHOPPED GINGER

2 TEASPOONS SOY SAUCE

Soak the noodles in warm water to cover until softened, about 30 minutes; drain. Cut the noodles into 3-inch pieces. Place the noodles and spinach on a serving platter with the lamb, shrimp, and green onions. Cover and refrigerate until ready to cook.

In separate small serving bowls, whisk the dipping sauce ingredients until blended.

Plotting Your Fire Pot
**When purchasing a fire
pot or hot pot, be sure
to find one that is
functional and not
merely ornamental. To
prevent damage to the
pot, fill the moat with
hot broth before adding
the charcoal. Light the
charcoal outdoors in a
barbecue, then transfer
them to the fire pot.
Make sure your
windows are open for
ventilation. Unable to
find a traditional fire
pot? In a pinch, use an
electric wok, or a
portable gas burner
with a 4- to 5-inch deep
pot, or even a fondue
pot. The Cantonese
version is a large clay
pot over a portable
burner or coal-burning
stove.**

In a large pot, bring the stock, ginger, and rice wine to a boil over medium-
high heat. Reduce the heat to low; cover and simmer for 20 minutes.
Discard the ginger. Set a Mongolian fire pot or an electric wok in the center
of the table. Arrange the lamb platter and dipping sauces around the
cooking vessel. Pour the hot broth into the fire pot and adjust the heat so
the broth simmers gently. Each diner cooks his or her choice of ingredients
and seasons it with dipping sauce.

Sautéed Liver with Onions, Chinese-Style

No, you haven't opened up the wrong cookbook. We sauté liver with onions in China as well. A winning combination is a winning combination in any cuisine. The difference is in the sauce. A touch of soy, a dash of rice wine, and you have a new classic in the making.

Makes 4 servings

Marinade

2 TABLESPOONS CHINESE RICE WINE OR
   DRY SHERRY

2 TABLESPOONS CORNSTARCH

¼ TEASPOON SALT

¼ TEASPOON WHITE PEPPER

• • •

1 POUND CALF'S LIVER (BLANCHED AS
   DESCRIBED AT RIGHT, IF DESIRED)

Sauce

¼ CUP CHINESE RICE WINE OR
   DRY SHERRY

2 TEASPOONS WORCESTERSHIRE SAUCE

1 TEASPOON SOY SAUCE

½ TEASPOON SUGAR

• • •

1 TEASPOON CORNSTARCH DISSOLVED IN
   2 TEASPOONS WATER

1 TABLESPOON COOKING OIL

1 ONION, CHOPPED

1 SLICE BACON, CUT INTO ½-INCH
   PIECES

2 TABLESPOONS WATER OR CHICKEN
   STOCK (OPTIONAL)

SLIVERED GREEN ONIONS

De-livering Liver

Many cooks (and diners) refrain from calf's liver because of its texture. Here is a good tip: Blanch the liver in hot water until lightly firm but not tough, then go through the regular cooking process.

Combine the marinade ingredients in a bowl. Add the liver and stir to coat. Let stand for 30 minutes.

Combine the sauce ingredients in a pan. Bring to a boil over medium heat. Add the cornstarch mixture and cook, stirring, until the sauce boils and thickens. Reduce the heat to low and keep warm.

Place a wide frying pan over high heat until hot. Add the oil, swirling to coat the sides. Add the liver and cook until it reaches desired doneness, 2 to 4 minutes on each side. If the liver is blanched beforehand, shorten the cooking time to 1 to 2 minutes on each side. Remove the liver from the pan and keep warm.

Add the onion and bacon; cook, stirring, until the bacon is crisp and the onion becomes translucent, about 5 minutes. If the mixture appears dry, add a tablespoon or two of water or chicken stock.

Place the onion mixture on a serving platter. Thinly slice the liver and arrange over the onion mixture. Garnish with the green onions and serve with the sauce on the side.

TWICE-COOKED PORK

"Twice-cooked" refers to the two-step cooking process to create this dish. It does not mean that you will only want to cook this dish twice. Chances are, your guests will be asking for encores.

<u>Makes 4 to 6 servings</u>

1 POUND BONELESS PORK BUTT

1 CUP CHICKEN STOCK

2 TABLESPOONS COOKING OIL

8 SMALL DRIED RED CHILES

1 TABLESPOON CHOPPED GARLIC

8 OUNCES NAPA CABBAGE, CUT INTO
   BITE-SIZE PIECES

3 GREEN ONIONS, CUT INTO 1-INCH
   LENGTHS

2 TABLESPOONS HOISIN SAUCE

2 TEASPOONS DARK SOY SAUCE

2 TEASPOONS LIGHT SOY SAUCE

1/8 TEASPOON SALT

2 TEASPOONS CORNSTARCH DISSOLVED
   IN 1 TABLESPOON WATER

In a pan, combine the pork and chicken stock. Bring to a boil over high heat. Reduce the heat to low; cover and simmer until tender, 40 to 45 minutes. Remove the pork from the pan and let cool; reserve the stock. Cut the pork into thin slices.

Place a wok or wide frying pan over medium-high heat until hot. Add the oil, swirling to coat the sides. Add the chiles and garlic; cook, stirring, until fragrant, about 10 seconds. Add the pork and stir-fry for 1 minute. Add the cabbage and onions; stir-fry for 30 seconds.

Add the reserved stock, hoisin sauce, dark and light soy sauces, and salt. Cook until the cabbage is tender-crisp, about 3 minutes. Add the cornstarch mixture and cook, stirring, until the sauce boils and thickens.

Excess Cabbage

When I was growing up, cabbage was a regular guest at my family's dining table. In China, in addition to regular cabbage, we also grow napa cabbage. Both of these kinds have sweet, cream-colored stalks, and they are great in soups and braising dishes.

GOOD FORTUNE MEATBALLS

*In Eastern China, this classic dish is better known as Lion's Head
Meatballs because of the large size of the meatballs, and their
"manes" of napa cabbage. Since this is a symbolic dish often served
during Chinese New Year, I've renamed it Good Fortune Meatballs.*

Makes 4 to 6 servings

10 FRESH SHIITAKE MUSHROOMS

Meatballs

12 OUNCES GROUND LEAN PORK

2 SLICES BACON, CHOPPED

1 EGG, LIGHTLY BEATEN

3 TABLESPOONS CORNSTARCH

1 TABLESPOON LIGHT SOY SAUCE

2 TEASPOONS FINELY CHOPPED
    CILANTRO

1 TEASPOON FINELY CHOPPED GINGER

• • •

COOKING OIL FOR DEEP-FRYING

1½ CUPS CHICKEN STOCK

2 TABLESPOONS CHINESE RICE WINE OR
    DRY SHERRY

1 TABLESPOON DARK SOY SAUCE

1 TABLESPOON LIGHT SOY SAUCE

12 OUNCES NAPA CABBAGE, CUT INTO
    4-INCH PIECES

1 CARROT, THINLY SLICED DIAGONALLY

16 SNOW PEAS, TRIMMED AND CUT IN
    HALF DIAGONALLY

2 TABLESPOONS CORNSTARCH
    DISSOLVED IN ¼ CUP WATER

Discard the mushroom stems and leave the caps whole.

Combine the meatball ingredients in a bowl; mix well. Divide the mixture
into 12 portions. Roll each portion into a ball.

In a wok, heat the oil for deep-frying to 350°. Deep-fry the meatballs,
one half at a time, turning frequently, until browned on all sides, 3 to
4 minutes. Remove and drain on paper towels.

Place the meatballs in a 2-quart pot. Add the stock, rice wine, and dark
and light soy sauces. Bring to a boil over high heat. Reduce the heat to
medium; cover and simmer for 10 minutes. Add the mushrooms, cabbage,
and carrot; cover and simmer for 10 minutes. Add the snow peas and
simmer until tender-crisp, 2 to 3 minutes. Add the cornstarch mixture and
cook, stirring, until the sauce boils and thickens.

Intro to Cilantro

**Cilantro also goes by
the names fresh
coriander and Chinese
parsley. Its distinctive
aromatic flavor goes
well with fish, poultry,
and red meat (how is
that for flexibility?). In
addition to using it as a
spice, it makes a good
garnish. Place a few
leaves at the side of the
serving platter, or float
them in a bowl of soup.
They are decorative as
well as aromatic.**

TOP RIGHT GOOD
FORTUNE MEATBALLS

RIGHT SAVORY
STEAMED SPARERIBS
(RECIPE PAGE 166)

SAVORY STEAMED SPARERIBS

Is there another way to cook spareribs besides baking and barbecuing? Try steaming. These ribs are steamed to tender perfection in a wok. Better allow for a few spare ribs; your guests will ask for seconds.

Makes 4 to 6 servings

Marinade

1 TABLESPOON CHINESE RICE WINE OR
   DRY SHERRY
1 TABLESPOON SOY SAUCE

* * *

1½ POUNDS PORK SPARERIBS, CUT
   BETWEEN THE BONES
4 TABLESPOONS COOKING OIL

Sauce

1 CUP WATER
¼ CUP SOY SAUCE
2 TABLESPOONS CHINESE RICE WINE OR
   DRY SHERRY
2 TABLESPOONS RED FERMENTED BEAN
   CURD
2 TABLESPOONS SUGAR

* * *

8 OUNCES BABY BOK CHOY, CUT
   LENGTHWISE INTO QUARTERS

Combine the marinade ingredients in a bowl. Add the ribs and stir to coat. Let stand for 30 minutes.

Place a wide frying pan over high heat until hot. Add 2 tablespoons of the oil, swirling to coat the sides. Add the ribs and cook until golden brown on all sides, about 4 minutes. Remove and drain on paper towels.

Combine the sauce ingredients in a wide frying pan. Cook, stirring, over high heat until the sauce boils. Add the ribs and stir to coat.

Prepare a wok for steaming (see page 212). Place the ribs on a heatproof dish. Cover and steam over high heat for 40 minutes. Place in the center of a serving platter.

Place a wok over high heat until hot. Add the remaining oil, swirling to coat the sides. Add the bok choy and stir-fry until tender-crisp, about 2 minutes. Arrange the bok choy around the ribs.

Letting Off Steam

After stir-frying, steaming is the second most popular cooking method in China. Steamer baskets made from bamboo are available in many department stores, and they come in all sizes. If you can't find them, improvise with a wok or a large-lidded pot. Heat 3 inches of water in the wok. Place the food on a heatproof glass dish and put it on a steaming rack, or atop two sets of crisscrossing chopsticks. Now comes the secret of steaming—cover it up! It won't work if you leave the cover off.

PINEAPPLE SWEET AND SOUR PORK

Here is a dish that needs no introduction. Years ago, I heard some of my friends define Chinese food as "anything sweet and sour." Asian culinary awareness has risen at least a hundredfold since then, but this delicious and easy-to-make Pineapple Sweet and Sour Pork remains a timeless classic.

Makes 4 servings

Marinade

2 TABLESPOONS OYSTER SAUCE

1 TABLESPOON CHINESE RICE WINE OR
   DRY SHERRY

• • •

12 OUNCES BONELESS PORK, CUT INTO
   1-INCH CUBES

1 EGG, LIGHTLY BEATEN

¼ CUP ALL-PURPOSE FLOUR

¼ CUP CORNSTARCH

½ TEASPOON BAKING POWDER

COOKING OIL FOR DEEP-FRYING

1 GREEN BELL PEPPER, SEEDED AND CUT
   INTO 1-INCH SQUARES

2 CUPS PINEAPPLE CHUNKS

½ CUP SWEET AND SOUR SAUCE

Variation on a Classic

Even a classic can use an improvement or two over time. With the current trend toward lighter cuisine, a perfectly suitable alternative to deep-frying the pork is stir-frying. For quicker stir-frying, cut the pork smaller than if it were to be deep-fried.

Combine the marinade ingredients in a bowl. Add the pork and stir to coat. Let stand for 30 minutes. Add the egg to the marinated pork and mix well.

In a bowl, combine the flour, cornstarch, and baking powder. Add the pork and toss to coat; shake to remove the excess. Let stand for 3 to 4 minutes.

Preheat the oven to 200°. In a wok, heat the oil for deep-frying to 375°. Deep-fry the pork, one half at a time, turning occasionally, until golden brown and cooked through, 3 to 4 minutes. Remove and drain on paper towels. Place the pork in a heatproof dish and keep warm in the oven while cooking the remaining pork.

Remove all but 1 tablespoon of oil from the wok. Place over medium-high heat until hot. Add the bell pepper; stir-fry until tender-crisp, about 1 minute. Add the pineapple and sauce; cook, stirring, until heated through. Add the cooked pork cubes and toss to coat. Place on a serving platter.

STIR-FRIED SHREDDED PORK WITH MUSHROOMS AND BEAN SPROUTS

Are pancakes only for breakfast? Not in my kitchen! And not with pancakes made from crispy noodles. For them I prefer a nice savory topping of stir-fried shredded pork or seafood. With slivers of black mushroom, it makes a wonderful meal—yes, even at breakfast.

Makes 4 servings

8 OUNCES PORK LOIN

Marinade

1 TABLESPOON CHINESE RICE
  WINE OR DRY SHERRY
2 TEASPOONS DARK SOY SAUCE
2 TEASPOONS LIGHT SOY SAUCE
1 TEASPOON CORNSTARCH

◆ ◆ ◆

4 DRIED BLACK (SHIITAKE)
  MUSHROOMS

Sauce

2 TABLESPOONS RICE VINEGAR
1½ TABLESPOONS LIGHT SOY
  SAUCE
2 TEASPOONS CHILE GARLIC SAUCE
2 TEASPOONS SESAME OIL
2 TEASPOONS SUGAR

◆ ◆ ◆

4 TABLESPOONS COOKING OIL
8 OUNCES FRESH CHINESE EGG
  NOODLES
COOKING OIL FOR DEEP-FRYING
1 RED JALAPEÑO CHILE, SEEDED
  AND CHOPPED
2 GREEN ONIONS, CHOPPED
1 STALK CELERY, THINLY SLICED
  DIAGONALLY
3 OUNCES FRESH MUNG BEAN
  SPROUTS

Thinly slice the pork, then cut the slices into thin strips. Combine the marinade ingredients in a bowl. Add the pork and stir to coat. Let stand for 30 minutes.

Soak the mushrooms in warm water to cover until softened, about 15 minutes. Reserve the mushroom soaking liquid. Discard the stems and thinly slice the caps. Combine the sauce ingredients in a bowl.

Preheat the oven to 200°. Place a wide nonstick frying pan over medium-high heat until hot. Add 1 tablespoon of the oil, swirling to coat the sides. Spread half the noodles over the bottom of the pan. Press the noodles into a firm pancake about 8 inches wide. Cook until the bottom is golden brown, about 5 minutes. With a wide spatula, carefully turn the pancake over. Add 1 more tablespoon of oil and cook until the other side is golden brown, about 3 minutes longer. Place the noodles on a large heatproof serving platter and keep warm in the oven. Repeat with the remaining oil and noodles.

In a wok, heat the oil for deep-frying to 350°. Deep-fry the pork, stirring to separate, for 1½ minutes. Remove and drain on paper towels. Remove all but 1 tablespoon of oil from the wok. Place over high heat until hot. Add the jalapeño and green onions; cook, stirring, until fragrant, about 10 seconds. Add the celery and stir-fry until tender-crisp, about 2 minutes. If the mixture appears dry, add a tablespoon or two of the reserved mushroom soaking liquid. Add the pork, mushrooms, and bean sprouts; stir-fry for 30 seconds. Add the sauce and cook until heated through.

Pour the shredded pork mixture over the noodles.

MEAT AND VEGETABLE WRAP

Most restaurants call it Mu Shu Pork. You can add any combination of meat and vegetables. It's the perfect dish for your next dinner party. Meat and Vegetable Wrap will keep your guests entertained offering each other tips on how to wrap the filling in perfect thin flour pancakes. If you can't find Mandarin pancakes in an Asian supermarket, ask for spring roll wrappers. Flour tortillas are also good substitutes.

Makes 6 to 8 servings

8 OUNCES BONELESS PORK

Marinade

2 TEASPOONS DARK SOY SAUCE

2 TEASPOONS LIGHT SOY SAUCE

2 TEASPOONS CORNSTARCH

4 DRIED BLACK (SHIITAKE) MUSHROOMS

2 OUNCES DRIED BEAN THREAD
   NOODLES

Sauce

2 TEASPOONS DARK SOY SAUCE

2 TEASPOONS LIGHT SOY SAUCE

1 TEASPOON SESAME OIL

2 TABLESPOONS COOKING OIL

2 TEASPOONS FINELY CHOPPED GARLIC

1 CARROT, JULIENNED

1 ZUCCHINI, JULIENNED

2 TABLESPOONS JULIENNED SICHUAN
   PRESERVED VEGETABLE

$1\frac{1}{2}$ TEASPOONS CORNSTARCH DISSOLVED
   IN 1 TABLESPOON WATER

12 TO 14 MANDARIN PANCAKES

HOISIN SAUCE

Fluff and Fold

Ever wonder how the Mandarin pancakes at Chinese restaurants always come hot and fluffy to your table? The answer is steam power, and you can harness it at home. Wrap the pancakes in a towel and steam them for 5 minutes. If you are using tortillas, you can steam them the same way, or heat them in a microwave.

Thinly slice the pork, then cut into thin strips. Combine the marinade ingredients in a bowl. Add the pork and stir to coat. Let stand for 30 minutes. Soak the mushrooms in warm water to cover until softened, about 15 minutes. Reserve the mushroom soaking liquid. Discard the stems and thinly slice the caps. Soak the bean thread noodles in warm water to cover until softened, about 15 minutes; drain. Cut the noodles into 4-inch lengths. Combine the sauce ingredients in a bowl.

Place a wok or wide frying pan over high heat until hot. Add the oil, swirling to coat the sides. Add the garlic and cook, stirring, until fragrant, about 10 seconds. Add the pork and stir-fry until lightly browned, about 2 minutes. Add the mushrooms, carrot, zucchini, and preserved vegetable; stir-fry until the carrot is tender-crisp, about 2 minutes. If the mixture appears dry, add a tablespoon or two of the reserved mushroom soaking liquid. Add the noodles and sauce and bring to a boil. Add the cornstarch mixture and cook, stirring, until the sauce boils and thickens.

Meanwhile, prepare a wok for steaming (see page 212). Wrap the pancakes in a kitchen towel, then place them on a heatproof dish. Cover and steam over high heat until heated through, about 5 minutes.

To eat, spread about a teaspoon of hoisin sauce on each pancake. Place 2 heaping tablespoons of the meat mixture along the length of the pancake. Wrap up and eat with your fingers.

To a large part of the world's population, rice is life! I grew up in Southern China, where rice has been the basic staple for countless generations. Even now, after all these years living in North America, I still feel a meal is incomplete without a bowl of steamed rice. And as much as I enjoy eggs and toast for breakfast, on a cold winter morning, I can never shake the craving for a simple bowl of Chinese Comfort Rice.

To cook rice, just add water and boil, right? Yes and no. Cooked rice can be much more than just plain boiled or steamed. For a change in texture, try my recipe for Rainbow Risotto, and for a rice dish that can easily be a meal in itself, heat up your wok and stir up the classic Yang Chow Fried Rice.

In Northern China, where the climate is cool and dry, wheat, not rice, is the most bountiful grain. Hence, my northern cousins are just as passionate about their noodles as I am about my daily rice. I owe to them many of the wonderful noodle recipes in this chapter —Chicken Chow Mein and Grandma's Sidewalk Noodles, to name just a couple.

Rice is life, and noodles are, too. Onward to rice and noodles, onward to life.

PAN-FRIED RICE NOODLES WITH CHAR SIU

Curry flavor and rice noodles go well together in a stir-fry. Rice noodles are wide noodles made from water and rice flour. If dried rice noodles are used, they need to be soaked and cooked in water before stir-frying.

Makes 4 servings

2 TABLESPOONS COOKING OIL

3 GREEN ONIONS, JULIENNED

4 OUNCES CHINESE BARBECUED PORK
(CHAR SIU), JULIENNED

4 OUNCES SMALL RAW SHRIMP,
SHELLED, DEVEINED, AND DICED

¼ ONION, SLICED

½ RED BELL PEPPER, SEEDED AND
JULIENNED

2 TABLESPOONS SOY SAUCE

4 TEASPOONS CURRY POWDER

2 TEASPOONS SESAME OIL

12 OUNCES FRESH OR DRIED RICE
NOODLES

1–2 TABLESPOONS WATER OR CHICKEN
STOCK (OPTIONAL)

Place a wok or wide frying pan over high heat until hot. Add the oil, swirling to coat the sides. Add the green onions; stir-fry for 10 seconds. Add the pork and the shrimp and stir-fry for 1 minute. Add the onion and cook for 1 minute. Add the bell pepper, soy sauce, curry powder, and sesame oil; cook for 1 minute. Reduce the heat to low and add the noodles; mix well. Cook until heated through. If the mixture appears dry, add water or chicken stock. Place on a platter and serve.

Rice in Your Noodles

Rice noodles are made of long-grain rice flour and water. The dry ones are either thin (labeled as "rice vermicelli") or wide (the width of fettuccine). Soak both kinds in warm water for about 15 minutes to soften before cooking. Fresh rice noodles come in folded sheets or as precut ribbons or spaghetti-thin strands. Find them in the refrigerated section of Asian markets and some supermarkets.

FRAGRANT NOODLES WITH BASIL

Those who think that noodles look and taste dull may be singing a different tune after one bowl of this spicy fragrant broth with noodles. A similar version (using hot bean paste and thick northern Chinese noodles) is served at traditional Chinese birthday celebrations. What an exciting way to start a new birth year!

Makes 4 servings

8 OUNCES GROUND LEAN PORK

2 TABLESPOONS SOY SAUCE

1 TABLESPOON DRIED SHRIMP

12 OUNCES FRESH CHINESE EGG NOODLES

1 TABLESPOON COOKING OIL

2 SHALLOTS, SLICED

1 CUP SHREDDED NAPA CABBAGE

¼ CUP CHICKEN STOCK

1 TABLESPOON HOISIN SAUCE

2 TEASPOONS CHILE GARLIC SAUCE

¼ CUP BASIL LEAVES

Combine the pork and soy sauce in a bowl; mix well. Let stand for 30 minutes. Soak the dried shrimp in warm water to cover until softened, about 20 minutes; drain.

Bring a pot of water to a boil. Add the noodles and cook according to the package directions. Drain, rinse with cold running water, and drain again. Place in a large serving bowl.

Place a wok or wide frying pan over high heat until hot. Add the oil, swirling to coat the sides. Add the shrimp, shallots, and pork; stir-fry for 1½ minutes. Add the cabbage; stir-fry for 1 minute. Add the stock, hoisin sauce, chile garlic sauce, and basil; cook, stirring, until heated through.

Pour the meat mixture over the noodles and toss to combine. Serve hot or cold.

FRAGRANT NOODLES WITH BASIL

PORK LO MEIN

This quick and delicious one-dish meal turns an ordinary lunch into a mini culinary feast. Now isn't this a great way to use your noodle?

Makes 4 to 6 servings

4 OUNCES BONELESS PORK

1 TEASPOON OYSTER SAUCE

Sauce

¾ CUP CHICKEN STOCK

2 TABLESPOONS CHINESE BLACK
   VINEGAR OR BALSAMIC VINEGAR

2 TABLESPOONS SOY SAUCE

1 TABLESPOON CHINESE RICE WINE OR
   DRY SHERRY

1 TABLESPOON SESAME OIL

1 TABLESPOON CORNSTARCH

2 TEASPOONS SWEET BROWN BEAN
   SAUCE

½ TEASPOON SUGAR

1 POUND FRESH CHINESE EGG NOODLES

2 TABLESPOONS COOKING OIL

1 TEASPOON FINELY CHOPPED GARLIC

1 CARROT, JULIENNED

1½ CUPS SHREDDED CABBAGE

3 OUNCES FRESH MUNG BEAN SPROUTS

1 TABLESPOON JULIENNED SICHUAN
   PRESERVED VEGETABLE

Thinly slice the pork, then cut the slices into thin strips. Place in a bowl and add the oyster sauce; stir to coat. Let stand for 30 minutes. Combine the sauce ingredients in a bowl.

Bring a pot of water to a boil. Add the noodles and cook according to the package directions. Drain, rinse with cold running water, and drain again.

Place a wok or wide frying pan over high heat until hot. Add the oil, swirling to coat the sides. Add the garlic and cook, stirring, until fragrant, about 5 seconds. Add the pork and stir-fry for 2 minutes. Add the carrot, cabbage, bean sprouts, and preserved vegetable; cook for 1 minute. Add the sauce and cook, stirring, until the sauce boils and thickens. Add the noodles and toss to coat.

SEAFOOD TRIO OVER CRISPY BROWNED NOODLES

A Chinese noodle shop serves more than noodles in soup. On the menu, you will find a variety of pan-fried noodle dishes listed under the chow mein and lo mein categories. One of my favorites is crisp, golden brown noodles topped with seafood. The recipe browns the noodles on top of the stove; if you prefer, brown them in the oven (see sidebar).

Makes 4 to 6 servings

4 DRIED BLACK (SHIITAKE) MUSHROOMS
4 OUNCES SQUID, CLEANED
8 OUNCES MEDIUM RAW SHRIMP,
    SHELLED AND DEVEINED
4 OUNCES SEA SCALLOPS, CUT IN HALF
    HORIZONTALLY
1 TABLESPOON CORNSTARCH
½ TEASPOON SALT

Sauce

⅔ CUP CHICKEN STOCK
1 TABLESPOON SOY SAUCE
1 TABLESPOON OYSTER SAUCE
1 TEASPOON SESAME OIL
1 TEASPOON CORNSTARCH

◆ ◆ ◆

8 OUNCES FRESH CHINESE EGG
    NOODLES
5 TABLESPOONS COOKING OIL
1 TABLESPOON FINELY CHOPPED GINGER
4 GREEN ONIONS, CUT INTO 2-INCH
    LENGTHS
4 OUNCES GARLIC CHIVES, CUT INTO
    2-INCH LENGTHS

Soak the mushrooms in warm water to cover until softened, about 15 minutes; drain. Discard stems and thinly slice the caps.

Leave the squid tentacles whole. Cut the bodies open and lightly score the inner side in a small crisscross pattern. Cut the body into 1½- to 2-inch pieces. Place the squid, shrimp, scallops, cornstarch, and salt in a bowl; stir to coat. Let stand for 15 minutes. Combine the sauce ingredients in another bowl.

Bring a pot of water to a boil. Add the noodles and cook according to the package directions. Drain, rinse with cold running water, and drain again.

Preheat the oven to 200°. Place a wide nonstick frying pan over medium-high heat until hot. Add 1 tablespoon of the oil, swirling to coat the sides. Spread half the noodles over the bottom of the pan. Press the noodles into a firm pancake about 8 inches wide. Cook until the bottom is golden brown, about 5 minutes. With a wide spatula, carefully turn the pancake over. Add 1 more tablespoon of oil and cook until the other side is golden brown, about 3 minutes longer. Place the noodles on a large

Oven-Browned Noodle Pancakes

The secret to perfect noodle pancakes is as close as your oven. Cook 1 pound of fresh Chinese egg noodles according to package instructions. Rinse under cold running water and drain. Preheat the oven to 500°. Place two 12-inch round pans in the oven. When the pans are very hot, brush 1 tablespoon cooking oil evenly on the surface of the pans, then spread the noodles evenly in a circle on the oiled surface; brush noodles with extra cooking oil. Bake until golden brown on top and bottom, 20 to 25 minutes.

heatproof serving platter and keep warm in the oven. Repeat with another 2 tablespoons of the oil and the remaining noodles.

Place a wok or wide frying pan over high heat until hot. Add the remaining 1 tablespoon of oil, swirling to coat the sides. Add the mushrooms, ginger, and green onions; stir-fry for 2 minutes. Add the squid, shrimp, and scallops; stir-fry for 2 minutes. Add the sauce and cook, stirring, until the sauce boils and thickens. Add the garlic chives; toss to coat. Cook until heated through. Spoon the seafood mixture over the noodles.

RICE STICKS WITH ROAST DUCK AND BABY BOK CHOY

A bowl of this brings back memories of my youth. The noodle shop was one of my favorite lunch hangouts, and rice sticks with slices of succulent roast duck on top was one of the reasons.

Makes 4 servings

12 OUNCES DRIED THIN RICE STICK
    NOODLES (¼ INCH WIDE)

1½ QUARTS CHICKEN STOCK

8 OUNCES BABY BOK CHOY, CUT
    LENGTHWISE INTO QUARTERS

½ TOMATO, SEEDED AND DICED

½ CHINESE ROAST DUCK, CUT INTO
    SERVING-SIZE PIECES

CILANTRO SPRIGS

Soak the noodles in warm water to cover until softened, about 15 minutes; drain. Bring a pot of water to a boil. Add the noodles and cook until tender but still slightly firm, 3 to 4 minutes. Drain, rinse with cold running water, and drain again. Divide the noodles among 4 soup bowls.

In a large pot, bring the stock to a boil over medium-high heat. Add the bok choy and cook until tender-crisp, about 1 minute. Add the tomato and remove the soup from the heat.

Ladle the broth over the noodles, then top with the bok choy, tomato, and roast duck. Garnish with the cilantro sprigs.

Zhejiang Noodles

Noodles served with meat sauce are not only Italian but also Chinese. Instead of tomato in the sauce, we use hoisin sauce and chile garlic sauce. For the meat, use ground lean pork, beef, or turkey.

Makes 4 to 6 servings

Sauce

1 CUP CHICKEN STOCK

3 TABLESPOONS HOISIN SAUCE

1 TABLESPOON CHINESE RICE WINE OR
  DRY SHERRY

2 TEASPOONS CHILE GARLIC SAUCE

◆ ◆ ◆

1 POUND FRESH CHINESE EGG NOODLES

1 TABLESPOON SESAME OIL

2 TABLESPOONS COOKING OIL

3 CLOVES GARLIC, FINELY CHOPPED

8 OUNCES GROUND LEAN MEAT

1 TABLESPOON CORNSTARCH DISSOLVED
  IN 2 TABLESPOONS WATER

2 GREEN ONIONS, SLIVERED

2 CARROTS, JULIENNED

½ CUCUMBER, JULIENNED

Combine the sauce ingredients in a bowl.

Bring a pot of water to a boil. Add the noodles and cook according to the package directions. Drain, rinse with cold running water, and drain again. Place in a bowl and add the sesame oil; toss to coat.

Place a wok or wide frying pan over high heat until hot. Add the oil, swirling to coat the sides. Add the garlic and cook, stirring, until fragrant, about 10 seconds. Add the meat and cook, stirring, until the meat is browned and crumbly, about 5 minutes. Add the sauce and bring to a boil. Add the cornstarch mixture and cook, stirring, until the sauce boils and thickens.

Place the noodles in individual serving bowls. Spoon the meat sauce over the noodles. Arrange the green onions, carrots, and cucumber on top.

GRANDMA'S SIDEWALK NOODLES

In China, noodles are a common snack food sold in the streets. My grandma ran a mobile noodle stand right outside her house and sometimes she actually carried the whole "kitchen" on her back as she went off to peddle her delicious soup noodles. Luckily for us, we can now enjoy the same noodles indoors, and without the weight of the kitchen on our back!

Makes 4 servings

Marinade

2 TABLESPOONS CHINESE RICE WINE OR
    DRY SHERRY

1 TABLESPOON OYSTER SAUCE

◆ ◆ ◆

8 OUNCES GROUND LEAN PORK

Sauce

½ CUP CHICKEN STOCK

¼ CUP SESAME SEED PASTE

3 TABLESPOONS SOY SAUCE

2 TABLESPOONS RICE VINEGAR

1 TEASPOON DRIED RED PEPPER FLAKES

½ TEASPOON SUGAR

◆ ◆ ◆

12 OUNCES FRESH CHINESE EGG
    NOODLES

2 TABLESPOONS COOKING OIL

CHOPPED SICHUAN PRESERVED
    VEGETABLE

CHOPPED UNSALTED ROASTED PEANUTS

Combine the marinade ingredients in a bowl. Add the pork and mix well. Let stand for 30 minutes. Combine the sauce ingredients in a bowl and whisk until blended.

Bring a pot of water to a boil. Add the noodles and cook according to the package directions. Drain, rinse with cold running water, and drain again. Place the noodles in a large serving bowl.

Place a wok or wide frying pan over high heat until hot. Add the oil, swirling to coat the sides. Add the pork and stir-fry for 2 minutes. Add the sauce and cook until heated through and pork is cooked. Pour the meat mixture over the noodles and garnish with the Sichuan preserved vegetable and peanuts.

Uncle Yan's Secret Meat Sauce

Fried noodles always give me a taste of home, so it was a great comfort when I came across this wonderful dish in my uncle's restaurant in Hong Kong. Follow the recipe and you can have this taste of home at home. Serve the sauce over Crispy Browned Noodles or Oven-Browned Noodle Pancakes (page 176).

Makes 4 servings

8 OUNCES GROUND LEAN PORK

1 TABLESPOON OYSTER SAUCE

Sauce

1 CUP CHICKEN STOCK

2 TABLESPOONS HOISIN SAUCE

1 TABLESPOON SOY SAUCE

1 TABLESPOON WORCESTERSHIRE SAUCE

1 TEASPOON SESAME OIL

1 TABLESPOON COOKING OIL

2 OUNCES CHINESE SAUSAGE
  (*LOP CHEONG*), COARSELY CHOPPED

1 TEASPOON FINELY CHOPPED GARLIC

1/2 TEASPOON DRIED RED PEPPER FLAKES

1/2 CUP COARSELY CHOPPED WATER
  CHESTNUTS

2 GREEN ONIONS, FINELY CHOPPED

2 1/2 TEASPOONS CORNSTARCH DISSOLVED
  IN 5 TEASPOONS WATER

OVEN-BROWNED NOODLE PANCAKES
  (SEE PAGE 176)

Combine the pork and oyster sauce in a bowl; mix well. Let stand for 30 minutes. Combine the sauce ingredients in a bowl.

Place a wok or wide frying pan over high heat until hot. Add the oil, swirling to coat the sides. Add the sausage, garlic, and pepper flakes; stir-fry for 1 minute. Add the pork and stir-fry until lightly browned and crumbly, about 2 minutes. Add the water chestnuts and green onions; cook for 1 minute. Add the sauce and bring to a boil. Add the cornstarch mixture and cook, stirring, until the sauce boils and thickens. Pour the meat mixture over the noodles and serve.

CHICKEN CHOW MEIN

Throughout my travels, I have discovered that there are probably as many versions of Chicken Chow Mein as there are Chinese restaurants. Chow Mein simply means stir-fry noodles; my recipe is a back-to-basics one.

Makes 4 to 6 servings

1 BONELESS, SKINLESS CHICKEN
   BREAST, THINLY SLICED
2 TABLESPOONS OYSTER SAUCE

Sauce

3 TABLESPOONS SOY SAUCE
2 TABLESPOONS HOISIN SAUCE
2 TABLESPOONS RICE VINEGAR
2 TABLESPOONS CHINESE RICE WINE OR
   DRY SHERRY
1 TABLESPOON SESAME OIL

• • •

1 POUND FRESH CHINESE EGG NOODLES
2 TABLESPOONS COOKING OIL
1 TEASPOON FINELY CHOPPED GINGER
1 LEEK, JULIENNED
1 RED BELL PEPPER, SEEDED AND
   JULIENNED

Place the chicken in a bowl and add the oyster sauce; stir to coat. Let stand for 15 minutes. Combine the sauce ingredients in a bowl.

Bring a pot of water to a boil. Add the noodles and cook according to the package directions. Drain, rinse with cold running water, and drain again.

Place a wok or wide frying pan over high heat until hot. Add the oil, swirling to coat the sides. Add the ginger and cook, stirring, until fragrant, about 5 seconds. Add the chicken and stir-fry for 2 minutes. Add the leek and bell pepper; cook for 1 minute. Add the sauce and cook until heated through and chicken is cooked. Add the noodles and toss to coat.

What Do You "Mein"?

The term chow mein literally means pan-fried or stir-fried noodles. Sometimes it is also referred to as *lo mein,* which means tossed egg noodles, or cooked noodles stir-fried along with meat and vegetables. In a Cantonese noodle shop, *lo mein* refers to a plate of boiled noodles served with a bowl of broth on the side. Thicker white noodles made from rice are called *fun,* and *chow fun* when they are stir-fried.

CHINESE COMFORT RICE

Americans may have their morning cereal, but when it comes to a breakfast of champions, we Chinese have congee, *a steaming bowl of creamy rice soup. It is the way millions (more accurately hundreds of millions) of Chinese start their day. How can a plain bowl of rice soup create such excitement? One word . . . toppings! We add slivered ginger, chopped green onions, Chinese pickled vegetables, and chopped roasted nuts on top.*

Makes 4 to 6 servings

³⁄₄ CUP LONG-GRAIN RICE
1 TEASPOON COOKING OIL
¹⁄₂ TEASPOON SALT
3 QUARTS CHICKEN STOCK

In a bowl, combine the rice, oil, and salt; mix well. Let stand for 15 minutes.

Place the rice mixture in a large pot. Add the stock and bring to a boil over high heat. Reduce the heat to low; cover and simmer, stirring occasionally, until the rice is soft and creamy, about 1¹⁄₂ hours. Add any leftover meat or seafood to make your own rice soup.

Steamed Rice

Long-grain rice is one of China's most basic foods. It is the least starchy of all the kinds of rice, and it cooks up dry and fluffy, with grains that separate easily. These characteristics make it ideal for stir-fry recipes.

To make 3 cups of steamed rice, combine ³⁄₄ cup long-grain rice with 1¹⁄₂ cups water in a medium pan. Bring to a boil over medium-high heat. Reduce the heat to low; cover and simmer until the water has evaporated and the rice is tender, 13 to 15 minutes. Remove from the heat and let stand, covered, for 5 minutes. Fluff with a fork or spoon before serving.

YANG CHOW FRIED RICE

You may want to call this dish "ultimate fried rice," or "rice for all occasions." Shrimp, bacon, barbecued roast pork, eggs, and vegetables make this a rice dish that can be served as a one-dish meal.

Makes 4 to 6 servings

Seasonings

2 TABLESPOONS SOY SAUCE

1½ TEASPOONS SESAME OIL

⅛ TEASPOON WHITE PEPPER

◆ ◆ ◆

3 TABLESPOONS COOKING OIL

2 EGGS, LIGHTLY BEATEN

1 SLICE BACON, DICED

¼ ONION, CHOPPED

1 OUNCE DICED CHINESE BARBECUED
   PORK (CHAR SIU)

3 CUPS COOKED LONG-GRAIN RICE

1 CUP SHREDDED LETTUCE

2 OUNCES SMALL COOKED SHRIMP,
   DICED

3 TABLESPOONS FROZEN PEAS AND
   CARROTS, THAWED

1–2 TABLESPOONS WATER OR CHICKEN
   STOCK (OPTIONAL)

Combine the seasoning ingredients in a bowl.

Place a 8- to 9-inch nonstick omelet pan over medium heat until hot. Add ½ tablespoon of the oil, swirling to coat the sides. Add the eggs and cook without stirring. As the edges begin to set, lift with a spatula and shake or tilt to let the eggs flow underneath. When the eggs no longer flow freely, turn them over and brown lightly on the other side. Slide the omelet onto a cutting board. Cut into strips about ¼ inch wide.

Place a wok or wide frying pan over high heat until hot. Add the remaining oil, swirling to coat the sides. Add the bacon, onion, and barbecued pork; stir-fry for 1 minute. Add the rice, lettuce, shrimp, and peas and carrots; stir-fry for 2½ minutes. If the mixture appears dry, add a tablespoon or two of water or chicken stock. Add the seasonings and mix well. Add the omelet strips and cook until heated through.

Firming Up

Freshly cooked long-grain rice is somewhat sticky and a bit too soft to fry in a wok or pan. My suggestion is to cook the rice ahead of time and store it overnight in the refrigerator. It will be nice and firm and ready for stir-frying the next day. Another tip is to stir-fry all the other ingredients first over medium heat, then add the rice. This prevents the rice from burning and sticking.

CURRY-FLAVORED CHICKEN RICE

Chinese chefs don't usually add nuts to fried rice, but on a visit to Sydney, Australia, one of the local chefs introduced me to it, and a jolly good idea from Down Under it was. Roasted cashew nuts taste just as good in fried rice north of the Equator.

Makes 4 servings

4 OUNCES BONELESS, SKINLESS
   CHICKEN, CUT INTO ¼-INCH PIECES
1 TABLESPOON OYSTER SAUCE

Seasonings

2 TABLESPOONS SOY SAUCE
2 TEASPOONS SESAME OIL
2 TEASPOONS CURRY POWDER

1 TABLESPOON COOKING OIL
½ ONION, FINELY CHOPPED
3 CUPS COOKED LONG-GRAIN RICE
4 GREEN ONIONS, FINELY CHOPPED
1–2 TABLESPOONS WATER OR CHICKEN
   STOCK (OPTIONAL)
⅔ CUP UNSALTED ROASTED CASHEWS,
   CHOPPED
½ CUP CRUSHED PINEAPPLE

Place the chicken in a bowl and add the oyster sauce; stir to coat. Let stand for 15 minutes. Combine the seasoning ingredients in a bowl.

Place a wok or wide frying pan over high heat until hot. Add the oil, swirling to coat the sides. Add the chicken and stir-fry for 2 minutes. Add the onion and stir-fry for 1 minute. Add the rice and green onions; stir-fry for 2 minutes. If the mixture appears dry, add a tablespoon or two of water or chicken stock. Add the seasonings and mix well. Add the cashews and pineapple; cook until heated through.

Hurry Curry

Indian curries are slowly cooked in a mixture of yogurt (Northern Indian) or coconut milk (Southern Indian). In Chinese cooking, curry is used as a flavor accent in vegetable and meat dishes as well as in rice, noodles, and dumplings.

FAMILY-STYLE CHICKEN AND RICE

My Latin American friends have a wonderful recipe for chicken cooked in rice, which they call arroz con pollo. *Here is a Chinese version that is the favorite one-pot meal of the Yan family.*

Makes 4 servings

6 DRIED BLACK (SHIITAKE) MUSHROOMS

8 OUNCES BONELESS, SKINLESS CHICKEN, CUT INTO 1/4-INCH PIECES

2 TABLESPOONS OYSTER SAUCE

Seasonings

2 TABLESPOONS DARK SOY SAUCE

1 TEASPOON SESAME OIL

1 1/2 CUPS LONG-GRAIN RICE

2 TABLESPOONS COOKING OIL

1 TABLESPOON CHOPPED SHALLOT

2 TEASPOONS FINELY CHOPPED GINGER

2 1/2 CUPS CHICKEN STOCK

4 OUNCES CHINESE SAUSAGES (*LOP CHEONG*)

2 GREEN ONIONS, SLIVERED

CILANTRO SPRIGS

Soak the mushrooms in warm water to cover until softened, about 15 minutes; drain. Discard the stems and cut the caps into quarters.

Place the chicken in a bowl and add the oyster sauce; stir to coat. Let stand for 15 minutes. Combine the seasoning ingredients in a bowl.

Place the rice in a rice cooker. (All Asian households have a rice cooker and I encourage using one; if you do not have one available, refer to page 185 for directions on how to make rice without a rice cooker.) Rinse 2 to 3 times with cold running water to remove excess starch and any foreign particles; drain. If using prepared converted rice, there is no need to rinse.

Place a wok or wide-frying pan over medium-high heat until hot. Add the oil, swirling to coat the sides. Add the shallot and ginger; cook, stirring, until fragrant, about 10 seconds. Add the chicken and cook until browned on all sides, about 2 minutes.

Place the chicken mixture and mushrooms in the rice cooker; mix well. Add the stock and mix well. Cook the rice according to the manufacturer's instructions. About 5 minutes before the rice is cooked, place the sausages and green onions on the rice. Cover and continue cooking. Pour the seasonings over the rice and garnish with the cilantro sprigs.

RAINBOW RISOTTO

What could be better than serving rice in a hearty risotto? The seafood flavor is slowly cooked into the rice, making it rich and tasty. This is perfect comfort food.

Makes 4 to 6 servings

14 OUNCES BONELESS CHICKEN THIGHS,
    CUT IN HALF
2 TABLESPOONS OYSTER SAUCE
2 OUNCES DRIED SHRIMP (OPTIONAL)
1 TABLESPOON COOKING OIL
2 TEASPOONS FINELY CHOPPED GARLIC
2 TEASPOONS FINELY CHOPPED GINGER
4 OUNCES CHINESE SAUSAGES *(LOP
    CHEONG)*, CUT INTO 1-INCH PIECES
½ ONION, CUT INTO 1-INCH PIECES

1 CUP LONG-GRAIN RICE
1 QUART CHICKEN STOCK
4 OUNCES SMALL HARD-SHELL CLAMS,
    WELL SCRUBBED
4 OUNCES FIRM WHITE FISH FILLET, CUT
    INTO 1-INCH PIECES
4 OUNCES MEDIUM RAW SHRIMP,
    WITH SHELLS
1 RED BELL PEPPER, SEEDED AND CUT
    INTO 1-INCH SQUARES
SLICED GREEN ONIONS

Place the chicken in a bowl and add the oyster sauce; stir to coat. Let stand for 15 minutes. Soak the dried shrimp in warm water to cover until softened, about 5 minutes; drain.

Place a wok or wide frying pan over high heat until hot. Add the oil, swirling to coat the sides. Add the garlic and ginger; cook, stirring, until fragrant, about 10 seconds. Add the chicken, dried shrimp, sausages, and onion; stir-fry for 1 minute. Add the rice, then the stock; mix well. Bring to a boil. Reduce the heat to medium; cover and simmer for 20 minutes. If you like a thicker risotto, simmer a little longer. Add the clams, fish, shrimp, and bell pepper; continue cooking for 10 minutes. Remove the wok from the heat and let stand for 5 minutes. Sprinkle the green onions over the rice and serve.

Symbolism of Rice

In China, rice symbolizes nourishment and well-being. Spilling rice is therefore bad luck, and serving badly cooked rice to a guest is an insult. There is an old belief that every grain of rice left behind in your bowl will be another freckle on the face of your future spouse. Is it any wonder that we Chinese clean our rice bowls with such vigor?

TEN-MINUTE WONTON SOUP

Get your stopwatch ready because it's time to make Ten-Minute Wonton Soup. Lay out your ingredients ahead of time and you should be serving up a steamy bowl of Wonton Soup in ten minutes or less. Went overtime on the first go? Don't worry, part of the fun here is in the practice.

Makes 6 to 8 servings

24 FROZEN WONTONS, POTSTICKERS, OR DUMPLINGS, THAWED

1½ QUARTS CHICKEN STOCK

2 SLICES GINGER, JULIENNED

2 OUNCES SLICED BAMBOO SHOOTS

¼ CUP SLICED WATER CHESTNUTS

½ TEASPOON SESAME OIL

⅛ TEASPOON WHITE PEPPER

4 OUNCES CHINESE BARBECUED PORK (*CHAR SIU*), THINLY SLICED

4 OUNCES MEDIUM COOKED SHRIMP, SHELLED AND DEVEINED

THINLY SLICED GREEN ONION

SLICED RED JALAPEÑO CHILE

Bring a pot of water to a boil. Add the wontons, half at a time, and cook until they begin to float, about 5 minutes. Remove and drain. To prevent the cooked wontons from sticking together, place them in a bowl of cold water.

In a large pot, bring the stock and ginger to a boil over medium-high heat. Add the bamboo shoots, water chestnuts, sesame oil, and pepper; cook for 1 minute.

Arrange several wontons, barbecued pork slices, and shrimp in individual soup bowls. Ladle the soup over all, then garnish with the green onion and jalapeño.

Wor Story

In Chinese, *wor* means a large stockpot. Hence, *wor wonton* refers to a large pot of wonton soup to which the chefs add all kinds of meats and vegetables. In some Chinese restaurants, you may find this listed as Special Wonton Soup or House Special Wonton Soup. Ask the waiter if it's Wor Wonton. He will be most impressed.

The perfect ending to a Chinese meal could be as simple as a plate of fresh seasonal fruits. Traditional Chinese desserts are sweet but not laden with cream, butter, or white sugar, as many Western desserts are. Many Chinese chefs like to use a variety of nuts as well as fruits such as lychee, banana, orange, mango, melon, pear, and pineapple.

Instead of baking desserts like cakes and cookies, we grind walnuts, peanuts, sesame seeds, and almonds, and make bowls of steamy sweet soups from them.

Over the years, Western desserts have made inroads into Chinese kitchens, so it is not uncommon to find European-style baked goods along with more traditional pastries in a Chinese bakery. Many in the West have the misconception that the Chinese don't have much of a sweet tooth. Quite the contrary. Special dessert restaurants are found all over mainland China, Hong Kong, Taiwan, and Singapore, and all the way to London, New York, Toronto, and Sydney.

In this chapter, I have included some of the most popular dessert recipes. Practice making them, and maybe your kitchen will become known as the next dessert restaurant.

COCONUT TARTS

What do you think of when someone mentions "tarts"? Personally I think of an oven-fresh, sweet, coconut flake–filled, buttery treat. That may sound like a mouthful . . . but oh what a delicious mouthful it is!

Makes 16 tarts

Filling

2 CUPS SWEETENED SHREDDED
  COCONUT

1 CUP EVAPORATED MILK

1/2 CUP UNSALTED ROASTED PEANUTS,
  CHOPPED

1 EGG

1/4 CUP BUTTER, MELTED AND COOLED

• • •

DOUBLE-CRUST PASTRY DOUGH
  (HOMEMADE OR STORE BOUGHT)

Preheat the oven to 350°.

Combine the filling ingredients in a bowl; mix well.

Roll half of the pastry between two sheets of plastic wrap until 1/8-inch thick. Cut into eight 3 1/2-inch circles. Press the circles into greased 2 1/2-inch muffin pan cups or tart pans. Stir the coconut mixture; fill the cups evenly. Repeat with the remaining pastry to make a total of 16 tarts.

Bake the tarts until golden brown, 25 to 30 minutes. If necessary, cover the tarts with foil after 20 to 25 minutes to prevent excess browning.

Let Them Eat Cake

Western-style bakeries are very popular in Hong Kong as well as other Asian cities. In addition to creamy cakes and sweet tarts and cookies, these bakeries offer an interesting hybrid of East/West buns and pastries—meat-filled turnovers, curried beef buns, cocktail buns, and cream-filled buns with coconut toppings, just to name a few. Today, Asian bakeries are popping up internationally, probably in a Chinatown near you. Be adventurous on your visit. Remember, not even the Chinese live on bread alone.

HAPPY SESAME SEED COOKIES

Anyone will love these cookies. Surprise: they're not baked in an oven but are deep-fried to become golden balls. Why do I call these cookies "happy"? Try one and see if you don't put on a broad smile.

Makes about 20 cookies

Dough

2 TABLESPOONS SHORTENING, AT ROOM
    TEMPERATURE

¾ CUP SUGAR

1 EGG, LIGHTLY BEATEN

¼ CUP WATER

2 CUPS ALL-PURPOSE FLOUR

2 TEASPOONS BLACK SESAME SEEDS

1¼ TEASPOONS BAKING POWDER

• • •

1 EGG, LIGHTLY BEATEN WITH
    1 TABLESPOON WATER

¾ CUP WHITE SESAME SEEDS

COOKING OIL FOR DEEP-FRYING

In a mixing bowl, beat the shortening and sugar until creamy. Add the egg and water; mix well. Add the flour, black sesame seeds, and baking powder; mix just until the dough comes together.

Roll the dough into a long cylinder; cut into 20 pieces. To make each cookie, roll each piece into a ball, then dampen with the egg-water mixture. Roll in the white sesame seeds to coat; set aside.

In a wok, heat the oil for deep-frying to 325°. Add half the balls at a time and cook, turning occasionally, until the surface cracks, 30 seconds to 1 minute. After the balls open, raise the heat to 350°; cook, turning, until the balls turn golden brown, 1 to 2 minutes longer. Remove and drain on paper towels. Serve at room temperature.

Turn Up the Heat, Slowly

Don't drop this cookie dough into very hot oil. Start your deep-frying at a lower temperature, and only turn up the heat towards the end. The fat in the dough cooks the dough from the inside so the dough will rise and brown properly. High heat will only burn the cookies before they're fully cooked in the center.

ALMOND CREAM

I've been told that my eyes are the fine shape of almonds. They most certainly light up every time they see this molded almond dessert. A few more helpings of this and my eyes will be shaped like lightbulbs.

Makes 4 servings

¼ CUP COLD WATER

1 ENVELOPE UNFLAVORED GELATIN

1 (11-OUNCE) CAN MANDARIN ORANGES
   IN SYRUP

¼ CUP SUGAR

1½ CUPS EVAPORATED MILK

¾ TEASPOON ALMOND EXTRACT

Pour the cold water into a bowl. Sprinkle the gelatin over the water. Let stand until softened, about 5 minutes. Drain the oranges, reserving the syrup. Set aside the orange sections for garnish. Add enough water to the reserved syrup to make ³/4 cup.

Combine the syrup and sugar in a pan. Cook, stirring, over medium-low heat until the sugar dissolves. Add the softened gelatin; stir until it dissolves, 3 to 4 minutes. Remove from the heat. Stir in the evaporated milk and almond extract. Pour into 4 individual dessert bowls. Cover and refrigerate until firm, 3 to 4 hours, or overnight.

To loosen the desserts, warm the base of each bowl in a bowl of warm water. Place a serving plate over the dessert bowl, then invert to unmold. Garnish with the orange sections.

Got Milk?

Evaporated milk, both sweetened and unsweetened, is very popular in Asia. This dates back to the time when refrigeration was not commonly available. Asians developed a taste for evaporated milk, and not just in their morning and afternoon tea. Today, many Asian recipes include this canned standby.

BAKED GINGER CUSTARD

For a change of pace (and taste), here is an interesting Asian variation on a traditional custard, prepared with a fine touch of ginger and coconut.

Makes 4 servings

½ CUP WATER

3 TABLESPOONS FINELY CHOPPED
  GINGER

6 TABLESPOONS SUGAR

2 EGGS, LIGHTLY BEATEN

½ CUP EVAPORATED MILK

½ CUP UNSWEETENED COCONUT MILK

4 TEASPOONS FINELY CHOPPED
  CRYSTALLIZED GINGER

MINT SPRIGS

Preheat the oven to 325°.

Combine the water and ginger in a small pan; bring to a boil over medium-high heat. Reduce the heat to low; cover and simmer for 5 minutes. Strain through a fine sieve and discard the ginger. Let the ginger water cool.

Measure ⅓ cup of the ginger water back into the pan (save the rest for another use or discard). Add the sugar and cook, stirring, over medium heat until the sugar dissolves. Remove the pan from the heat and let cool.

To make the custard, combine the eggs, evaporated milk, and coconut milk in a bowl; whisk until blended. Add the ginger water syrup and blend well. Skim any bubbles from the top of the custard mixture with a spoon.

Place ½ teaspoon of the crystallized ginger in the bottom of 4 individual heatproof dessert bowls. Fill the bowls evenly with the custard. Place the bowls in a shallow roasting pan half-filled with hot water. Bake until the custard no longer jiggles in the center when gently shaken, 20 to 30 minutes.

To serve, sprinkle the remaining ginger over the custard tops and garnish with the mint sprigs. Serve warm or cold.

Milk from a Nut?

Coconut milk is commonly available in cans, but it isn't the same liquid that spills out when a fresh coconut is opened. That is coconut water. Coconut milk is actually extracted from the coconut meat. The meat is puréed with water, then the milk is pressed out.

Before opening a can of coconut milk, shake it well, because the cream tends to rise to the top after the can has been sitting on the shelf for a while.

SWEET WONTON PILLOWS

Don't worry, you won't fall asleep on these golden brown little pockets filled with peanuts and coconut. The only trouble is that they are so delicious everybody will want more . . . so get ready for a pillow fight!

Makes 24 pillows

Filling

2 TABLESPOONS PACKED BROWN SUGAR

2 TABLESPOONS UNSWEETENED
   SHREDDED COCONUT

2 TABLESPOONS CHOPPED UNSALTED,
   ROASTED PEANUTS

2 TABLESPOONS SESAME SEEDS

24 WONTON WRAPPERS

24 MINT LEAVES

1 EGG, LIGHTLY BEATEN

COOKING OIL FOR DEEP-FRYING

Combine the filling ingredients in a bowl. Place 1 teaspoon of filling in the center of a wonton wrapper; top with a mint leaf. Brush the edges of the wrapper lightly with the egg. Fold the wrapper in half diagonally over the filling to form a triangle. Squeeze out the air, then pinch the edges to seal.

In a wok, heat the oil for deep-frying to 350°. Add the triangles, a few at a time, and deep-fry until golden brown, 1 to 2 minutes. Remove the triangles and drain on paper towels.

LYCHEE ICE CREAM

Growing up in Southern China, I was a nut for lychees at an early age. One bite of this succulent fruit takes me back to my old house in Guangzhou, and it is summer all over again. Lychee ice cream is simply supreme.

Makes about 1 quart

1 (12-OUNCE) CAN LYCHEES IN SYRUP

1 QUART VANILLA ICE CREAM, SLIGHTLY
   SOFTENED

CHOPPED CRYSTALLIZED GINGER

Drain the lychees, reserving the syrup. Coarsely chop the lychees and place them with the syrup in a baking pan. Freeze until solid, about 2 hours.

Break the lychees and syrup into 2-inch pieces. Place the pieces with the ice cream in a food processor; process until blended. Pour into a 1½-quart container; freeze until firm.

To serve, scoop the ice cream into bowls and garnish with the ginger.

Mango Madness

As an alternative to ice cream with lychees, try making it with mangoes. Anyone who has visited the Philippines, Thailand, India, or Mexico will come home singing the praises of mangoes. While North American mangoes are bulkier and meatier, Asian mangoes are far sweeter and more fragrant, and can turn any ordinary dessert, salad, or salsa into a spectacular treat.

Sweet Wonton Pillows

SWEET FIRECRACKERS

For me, firecrackers always bring up images of Chinese New Year and other celebrations. Here's something that'll bring a bang to your dessert table. This colorful dessert is just perfect for any festive occasion.

Makes 16 pastries

Filling

½ CUP WALNUTS, FINELY CHOPPED

1 CUP DRIED MIXED FRUIT BITS
    (INCLUDES APPLES, APRICOTS,
    RAISINS, AND PEACHES) OR CHOPPED
    PITTED DATES

1 TABLESPOON FINELY CHOPPED ORANGE
    ZEST

¼ TEASPOON GROUND CINNAMON

2 SHEETS (1 POUND) PUFF PASTRY
    DOUGH

1 EGG, LIGHTLY BEATEN WITH
    1 TABLESPOON WATER

Preheat the oven to 350°. Spread the walnuts in a shallow baking pan. Toast, shaking the pan occasionally, until fragrant and golden brown, 3 to 5 minutes. Cool.

Increase the oven temperature to 375°. Combine the filling ingredients in a bowl.

Roll each sheet of puff pastry to 12 by 14 inches. Cut into 8 rectangles, each 3½ by 6 inches.

To make each firecracker, place 1 rounded teaspoon of the filling down the length of a rectangle, leaving a 1½-inch edge on both short sides. Brush the long sides with the egg mixture. Roll up tightly, pinching to seal. Pinch the ends tightly to resemble a firecracker; secure the pinched ends with a band of foil. Place on a baking sheet, seam side down. Repeat with remaining filling and dough. Brush tops with egg mixture.

Bake until golden brown, 10 to 12 minutes. Cool on a wire rack. Remove foil bands before serving.

Wrap It Up

As an alternative to puff pastry dough, try egg roll wrappers (look for them in an Asian grocery). And instead of baking the pastries, deep-fry them until golden brown, 1 to 2 minutes. Instead of the mixed fruit bits, you can substitute prunes or shredded coconut.

EIGHT TREASURES RICE PUDDING

How about a sweet treasure hunt at the end of a great meal? Serve this elegant and colorful Eight Treasures Rice Pudding and watch how anxiously your guests will dig their spoons in. A perfect dessert for a dinner party at home.

Makes 4 to 6 servings

2 CUPS SHORT-GRAIN (GLUTINOUS) RICE

3 CUPS COLD WATER

½ CUP SUGAR

1 TABLESPOON COOKING OIL

11 OUNCES LOTUS SEED PASTE, BEAN PASTE, OR ANY SWEET OR SAVORY FILLING

1 TABLESPOON CHOPPED CRYSTALLIZED GINGER

Eight Treasures

½ CUP TOASTED WALNUTS

6 DRIED RED DATES, SOAKED

4 MARASCHINO CHERRIES, CUT IN HALF

3 DRIED APRICOTS CUT INTO QUARTERS

¼ CUP DRIED MIXED FRUIT BITS (INCLUDES APPLES, APRICOTS, RAISINS, AND PEACHES)

Syrup

½ CUP WATER

¼ CUP UNSWEETENED COCONUT MILK (OPTIONAL)

1 TABLESPOON FRESHLY SQUEEZED LEMON JUICE

1 CUP SUGAR

• • •

2 TEASPOONS CORNSTARCH DISSOLVED IN 1 TABLESPOON WATER

Soak the rice in warm water to cover for 2 hours; drain. Combine the rice and the cold water in a pan; cook over medium-high heat until crater-like holes form. Reduce the heat to low; cover and cook for 15 to 20 minutes. Let cool. Combine the rice, sugar, and oil; stir to coat. Set aside.

Line the bottom and sides of two 1-quart heatproof bowls with plastic wrap. Layer half of the walnuts, red dates, maraschino cherries, and dried apricots on the bottom of one bowl to form a pattern. Layer one quarter of the rice over the pattern to set. Spread half of the lotus seed paste on top of the rice. Sprinkle half of the crystallized ginger over the lotus seed paste. Add another quarter of the rice to fill the bowl. Press down to pack the rice and lotus seed paste. Sprinkle half of the dried fruit bits on top of the rice. Repeat with the remaining ingredients for the second bowl.

Prepare a wok for steaming (see page 212). Place the filled bowls on a rack and steam for 10 minutes. Place a serving platter over each bowl; invert to unmold. Discard the plastic wrap.

Combine the syrup ingredients in a saucepan. Cook, stirring, over medium heat until the sugar dissolves. Add the cornstarch mixture and cook, stirring, until the sauce boils and thickens. Pour the sauce over the puddings and serve.

Take a Number

Not all numbers are created equal in Chinese culture. The number three rhymes with the word "life" or "to live" and is therefore a "good" number. Number four, on the other hand, is "bad" because it has the misfortune of rhyming with the word "death." Nine is a good number because it rhymes with "forever," a suggestion of long life. Number eight is the most sought after number because it rhymes with "riches," as in coming into a fortune.

Note: **If dried fruit mix is not available, use your own choice of cut-up dried fruit to make ¼ cup.**

Brown Sugar Coconut Ice Cream

Growing up in China, I never screamed much for ice cream, but I screamed plenty for brown sugar and rock sugar. Both were common sweetening agents (white sugar was less common back then) and in a pinch, a quick piece of candy or dessert for children. Now that I have discovered coconut ice cream, I can combine it with my childhood favorite brown sugar.

Makes 1 quart

1 TABLESPOON BUTTER

½ CUP UNSWEETENED SHREDDED
    COCONUT

2 CUPS MILK

2 EGGS

⅔ CUP PACKED BROWN SUGAR

1⅔ CUPS UNSWEETENED COCONUT MILK

½ TEASPOON VANILLA EXTRACT

Melt the butter in a small frying pan over medium heat. Add the coconut and cook, stirring frequently until golden brown, about 3 to 4 minutes. Set aside.

Bring the milk to a simmer in a pan. Do not allow to boil.

Whisk the eggs in a bowl. Gradually add the sugar, mixing well after each addition. Slowly stir in the hot milk. Mix until the sugar dissolves. Return the mixture to the pan. Cook, stirring, over medium-low heat until the thickened mixture coats the back of a spoon, about 10 to 12 minutes. Do not allow to boil.

Remove the pan from the heat and add the coconut milk and vanilla extract; whisk until blended. Strain the liquid and discard any pieces of egg yolk.

Transfer the mixture to an ice cream maker and freeze according to the manufacturer's instructions.

Note: **If you do not have an ice cream maker, freeze the mixture in a baking pan for 3 hours. Cut the mixture into small blocks. Transfer the blocks to a food processor fitted with a metal blade; process the mixture until creamy and smooth, about 1 minute. Serve immediately or place in a container and freeze until ready to serve.**

FRUIT COMPOTE WITH SWEET AND TANGY PLUM SAUCE

Why have a plain fruit salad when you can jazz it up with plum wine and ginger? The taste of plum with mandarin oranges, pineapple, and kiwi is a winning combination.

Makes 4 servings

¼ CUP PLUM WINE

3 TABLESPOONS PRESERVED GINGER IN SYRUP

1 TABLESPOON PLUM SAUCE

1 (20-OUNCE) CAN PINEAPPLE CHUNKS, DRAINED

1 (11-OUNCE) CAN MANDARIN ORANGES, DRAINED

3 KIWI, PEELED AND CUT INTO CHUNKS

MINT SPRIGS

In a serving bowl, combine the wine, preserved ginger and some of its syrup, and plum sauce; mix well. Add the pineapple, oranges, and kiwi; toss to coat. Garnish with the mint sprigs.

Preserving Ginger

If you can't buy preserved ginger, you can make your own. Cut peeled ginger into ⅛-inch slices to make ½ cup. Place in a small pan with ½ cup sugar and ½ cup water. Simmer until the ginger is tender-firm and the syrup is almost completely absorbed, 8 to 10 minutes. Refrigerate until needed.

CREAM OF ALMOND SOUP

Soup for dessert? Why not? In China, sweet soups are popular desserts, and specialty dessert cafes feature a variety of sweet soups like this one on their menus.

Makes 4 servings

2 TABLESPOONS SLIVERED ALMONDS
2 CUPS WATER
½ CUP PACKED BROWN SUGAR
¾ CUP ALMOND PASTE
½ CUP UNSWEETENED COCONUT MILK

6 TABLESPOONS EVAPORATED MILK
  OR HALF-AND-HALF
1 TABLESPOON PEANUT BUTTER
MINT LEAVES

Preheat the oven to 350°. Spread the almonds in a shallow baking pan. Toast, shaking the pan occasionally, until fragrant and golden brown, 5 to 10 minutes. Cool.

In a pan, combine the water and brown sugar. Cook, stirring, over medium-high heat until the sugar dissolves; let cool.

In a food processor or blender, process the almond paste, coconut milk, evaporated milk, and peanut butter until well blended. Add the sugar water and whirl until blended. Return the mixture to the pan; cook, stirring, over low heat until heated through. Serve, or refrigerate and serve cold. Garnish with the mint and toasted almonds.

Sweets for the Sweet

In trendy Hong Kong, there's been an explosion of dessert cafes, and the city's international hotels have picked up the trend and are offering dessert buffets with everything from sweet crepes to Italian cannoli to traditional Chinese sweet soups. What's the response to this all-sweets all-night adventure? On my last visit, tables were booked a week in advance. How's that for the sweet taste of success?

Sweet Potatoes with Candied Ginger

The taste of sweet potatoes brings back wonderful memories of my youth. One of my grandmother's favorite sweets was sweet potato and crunchy pine nuts in a light syrup. It was easy to prepare and nobody in our household could get enough of it. To make it even lighter and more interesting, I have added a variety of fresh fruits.

Makes 4 servings

2½ CUPS COLD WATER

1 POUND SWEET POTATOES, PEELED AND CUT INTO ½-INCH CUBES

¼ CUP SUGAR

3 TABLESPOONS CHOPPED CRYSTALLIZED GINGER

3 OUNCES LONGAN, CHOPPED

1 MANGO, PEELED, SEEDED, AND DICED

1 BANANA, PEELED AND CUT INTO ¼-INCH SLICES

¼ CUP TOASTED PINE NUTS

In a pan, combine the water and sweet potatoes and bring to a boil. Simmer for 10 minutes. Add the sugar and ginger; mix well. Continue cooking until the sweet potatoes are tender on the outside and slightly crunchy in the center, about 10 more minutes.

Spoon the sweet potato mixture into 4 shallow bowls. Top with longan, mango, banana, and pine nuts. Serve warm or at room temperature.

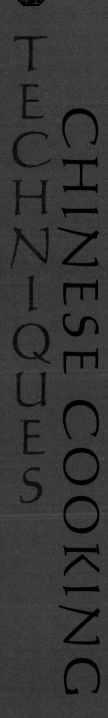

CHINESE COOKING TECHNIQUES

The Chinese Chef Knife
AN ALL-PURPOSE TOOL IN THE KITCHEN

About the Knife

The Chinese chef knife is my best friend. I use it to slice, dice, cube, and julienne. I use the butt of its handle to crush garlic, ginger, and salted black beans. I *do not,* however, use it to chop through chicken, heavy pork, and beef bones. The average Chinese chef knife is not designed for that task. Use a heavy meat cleaver. Or better yet, ask your friendly butcher to do it at the shop.

The larger, broad, rectangular shape and basic design for the Chinese knife has remained remarkably consistent over the centuries. The simplicity of the Chinese knife is a big reason for its endurance. The best way to pick out a good knife is by feel. The knife should be well balanced; not too light, and not too heavy. The best blades are made of high carbon stainless steel, which is easy to maintain and sharpen and keeps its edge for a good long time. Another feature of high carbon stainless steel is that it does not react with onion, garlic, or foods that are acid in nature. For the longest time, I could not find the right knife for my touch so I subsequently designed the ultimate chef's knife—the Martin Yan signature knife. In the cooking business, it's always nice to stay on the cutting edge.

Handling Your Knife

I hold my cleaver by sliding my hand forward until my thumb reaches one side of the blade and my index finger on the other. Use a firm grip on the handle; now curl the fingers of your other hand (so they are not exposed to the blade) and press down on the food that you are cutting. Use your first knuckles as a guide for your blade.

Techniques of the Knife

Instead of knives and forks, Chinese pick up food with a pair of chopsticks. To facilitate this, cut all the ingredients into bite-size pieces before cooking. The following cutting techniques are important in the preparation of a variety of Chinese dishes.

Slicing

Cut straight down with your blade at an even pace, as this helps to make the slices uniform in thickness. When slicing stalklike or cylindrical vegetables for stir-fry dishes (celery, carrots, etc.), do it on the diagonal. This will expose more of the surface of the vegetables, which quickens cooking time and allows flavors to be absorbed more readily.

Julienne (Matchstick) Cutting

First cut the ingredient into thin slices of the length that you desire, then stack these slices and cut down through the stacks lengthwise, to the width of a wooden matchstick.

Cubing, Dicing, and Mincing

To cut ingredients into cubes, first cut them into about ¾-inch slices, then cut the slices into ¾-inch sticks. Finally, cut across the sticks to make ¾-inch cubes. For dicing, same technique but smaller, ¼ to ½ inch, and for mincing, ¹/₁₆ inch. Yes, you can mince with your cleaver. The Chinese invented the cleaver long before we discovered the convenience of a food processor. For fine mincing, rock your cleaver blade back and forth, using the tip of the blade as a pivot, and cut until the ingredient reaches the desired fineness.

Crushing

A cleaver handle is more than a grip for the blade. It can also be used to crush garlic, ginger, or salted black beans. I crush them before cooking or adding to a marinade to better release their flavors. Another simple (and more dramatic) way to crush garlic and ginger is to place them on a cutting board and smack them with the broad side of your cleaver.

Meat Cutting

The best way to cut meat is to cut it across the grain, at a right angle to the direction of the fibers; this is particularly true for beef. For stir-fry dishes, I cut most of my meats into thin slices, which shortens the cooking time required.

Cooking Techniques

Organizing

Regardless of the type of cuisine, good organization is the key to success. Good organization is important across the board, from menu planning to procuring the right equipment and tools to assembling the right seasonal ingredients ahead of time. Begin cutting and marinating early. It will save a lot of time, not to mention tension and grief, later when your roomful of guests is waiting for the feast to commence. Plan the order in which you want to cook your dishes and lay out the tools required accordingly. Many sauces can be made ahead of time and warmed up when the time comes to serve. Cold dishes such as salads should have all of their ingredients sliced and diced ahead for last minute mixing and tossing. Start soups and slow-braising dishes hours ahead and they will be ready to serve when your quick-cook stir-fries are done. To sum it up, cook ahead, plan ahead, and you and your guests will have plenty of time to enjoy the delicious meal later.

Marinating

Marinating meat, poultry, and seafood before cooking is "de rigueur" in Chinese cooking. The marinating process is supposed to add flavor to your ingredients, not to tenderize them. Personally, I always marinate ahead of time and keep my ingredients refrigerated; this will save time when I am ready to cook. Usually 15 minutes of marinating is sufficient. A simple marinade is a mixture of soy sauce, cooking oil, cooking wine, sesame oil, oyster sauce, and a bit of cornstarch.

Stir-frying

Stir-frying is without a doubt the most popular method of cooking in Chinese cuisine, as it is a quick, easy, and healthy way of preparing food. The secret to a good stir-fry dish is high heat, quick motion, a good marinade, and ingredients cut to the right sizes (see page 210 for cutting techniques).

Heat up a wok or large frying pan (preferably one with a curved bottom) before adding cooking oil and seasonings like garlic and ginger. Next, add the main ingredient (meat, poultry, or seafood). Cook in the hot oil and seasonings, turning the ingredients rapidly with your

spatula. Remove the ingredients, and with the drippings, cook the vegetables. When cooking the vegetables, add the ones that require the longest cooking time, such as carrots, bell peppers, or onions, to the wok or pan first, then lighter vegetables such as snow peas and bean sprouts. When the vegetables are done, return the meat to the wok or pan and add a little cornstarch mixture to thicken the sauce. Off with the heat and dinner is served!

Steaming

Long before the first steam engine was invented in the West, the Chinese harnessed steam power in the kitchen. Steaming is a wonderful cooking method, for it allows your food to cook in its own juices, thereby retaining its natural flavors and nutritional properties. Note that steaming does not add oil or other fat to your dish.

Personally, I prefer traditional Chinese bamboo steamers. Their woven tops allow excess steam to escape without condensing and dripping back to the food. What's more, you can stack them, and that frees up other burners on the stove. For those who are "bamboo challenged," I recommend placing a small empty can (top and bottom removed) inside a large pan as a ring. Add water to about half way up the "ring" and on top of that, place your ingredients in a heatproof dish. Bring the water to a slow boil and cover. Instead of a ring, you may also do it the old Chinese way—on top of a pair of crossed chopsticks.

Traditional Chinese cooks often cook with medicinal herbs using a technique called double boiling. Double boiling is a form of steaming in which the ingredients (and herbs) are placed inside a covered earthenware casserole. The casserole is then placed in a larger pot with an inch of water inside. Cover the large pot and bring the water to a slow, simmering boil. This method requires several hours, giving the broth inside the casserole an intensely rich flavor.

Blanching

Blanching is a quick and efficient way to cook your vegetables. Blanching is simply submerging your vegetables, cut up to the desired size (see page 210), in boiling water for a short period, then extracting them and running cold water over them to stop the cooking process. Blanching the vegetables before stir-frying will shorten the cooking time required. Blanching can also remove that metallic taste from canned vegetables. In some Chinese restaurants, oil blanching is a common technique to seal the natural juices in meat.

Deep-frying

There are many models of conventional and electric deep-fryers available on the market, but personally I prefer the old-fashioned wok. To secure it on the burner (safety is the first concern in my kitchen), I put the wok on a ring stand, thus preventing the round-bottomed wok from tipping over during the frying process. I add about 2 to 2½ inches of oil, and I heat it up slowly. To control the temperature (usually specified in the recipes), I use a deep-frying thermometer. For the old-fashioned cooks, when small bubbles begin to rise in the oil, it is hot enough. Do not fry the food when the cooking oil is not at the right temperature. If it is too hot, your food will burn too quickly on the outside while leaving the inside uncooked, and if it is not hot enough, your food will take too long to cook, and it will absorb too much oil in the process.

I like to dry-coat my deep-frying ingredients with some cornstarch or flour. This will absorb any extra moisture and prevent oil from splattering. Slide your food into the oil gently, a few pieces at a time. Too many pieces in the fryer will lower the oil temperature and increase the cooking time. Turn the pieces from time to time to assure even cooking on all sides. When they are golden brown, remove them from the oil and drain them on a paper towel. I usually pat them down further with another towel to soak up excess oil.

Braising

Braising, a very popular cooking method in Chinese cuisine, is really a combination of two separate steps. First, the meat is browned (stir-fried) in a wok or a frying pan, which seals in the meat's natural juices. Then the wok is covered and the meat is allowed to simmer in a liquid. This will make the meat more tender and allow time for it to absorb the flavor of the cooking sauce.

Red Cooking

Red cooking is braising in a "red-cooking" sauce. Different chefs and restaurants boast about their own secret recipe, which is usually a mixture of soy sauce, dark soy sauce, spices, and other seasonings. The reddish brown color of the sauce gave origin to the name "red cooking." Often the red-cooking sauce is saved after each cooking process. It will be used as the base sauce for the next red-cooked dish. Chefs will add a splash of soy sauce here and a dash of seasoning there and off they go with another creation. Like a fine wine, red-cooking sauce gets better with age—richer and more flavorful with each cooking.

Roasting

In Chinese cuisine, roasting is not done over an open pit. Marinated meat is hung on hooks and "baked" inside a vertical roasting oven. In the old days, few homes in China were equipped with a baking oven, so roasting was more often done commercially in restaurants or delicatessens. But times have changed and so has technology. Today, many Chinese families roast (or bake) their own meat on a rack placed inside a baking pan. As in Western cooking, they may baste their meat with a marinade or pan juices.

Smoking

Not all smoking is bad for your health. In Chinese cooking, smoking is a way of adding flavor to meats, seafood, and poultry. Traditional Chinese recipes call for a traditional smoking oven, but you can recreate the effect by using a wok. For smoking ingredients, I mix black tea leaves, camphor chips, brown sugar, and some rice at the bottom of the wok. On top of that mixture, I place a rack on which I place the meat (precooked). Simply cover and turn up the heat. In minutes, the smoke inside the wok will permeate the meat, giving it a fragrant smoky flavor.

Microwaving

Technology marches on. A microwave oven is a necessity in today's kitchen. While it won't replace your wok or conventional oven (it didn't replace mine), it sure makes life easier when it comes to defrosting meat and vegetables. A tip on cutting meat that was frozen: Thaw it halfway to make cutting much easier. The microwave is by far the quickest and most energy-efficient way to reheat leftover steamed rice, noodles, and stir-fried dishes; selected dishes can also be prepared in the microwave. Place your food in a microwave container, or in a heatproof dish covered by a piece of plastic wrap.

ASIAN EGGPLANT

Both the Chinese and Japanese varieties are commonly available in your local Asian green grocer. Chinese eggplant are white to lavender in color; Japanese are light to dark purple. Both are sweet and do not need to be salted or soaked before cooking. There is no need to peel them as their skins are not tough and perfectly edible.

ASIAN PEAR

Also called apple pear. Sweet and juicy like a pear but with a crisp and crunchy texture like an apple. Asian pears are ideal for fruit as well as regular salads.

BAMBOO LEAVES, DRIED

A versatile wrapper for grilling, steaming, or boiling dishes. Bamboo leaves also impart an aromatic flavor to the food.

BAMBOO SHOOTS

The shoots of the bamboo are tender with a slightly sweet taste. Winter bamboo shoots are more desirable. Bamboo shoots are available mostly in cans—sliced or whole. Occasionally, fresh bamboo shoots are found in Asian stores.

BEAN CURD

See Tofu

BEAN SAUCE

See Sauces

BEAN SPROUTS

There are two common types: mung bean sprouts and the crunchier soy bean variety. Use them interchangeably. All sprouts are perishable and best used on the day of purchase, although they can be refrigerated for a couple of days.

BEAN THREAD NOODLES

See Noodles

BLACK BEANS, SALTED

Also called preserved or fermented black beans. They give food a pungent, smoky flavor that is a trademark of many dishes from Southern China. Salted black beans come in plastic packages or in cans. They should have a moist, soft texture, not hard and dried out. To reduce the salt content, soak the black beans in water before cooking.

BLACK BEAN SAUCE

See Sauces

BLACK MUSHROOMS

See Mushrooms

BOK CHOY

A very versatile leafy vegetable in Chinese cooking. This loose-leaved cabbage has thick white stalks and dark green leaves. Use it in stir-fry and braised dishes, as well as soups. Baby bok choy and Shanghai baby bok choy are two smaller, sweeter, and less fibrous varieties of bok choy that are available from your Asian grocer.

BOUILLON, SEAFOOD

No time to make your own fish stock? Dissolve 1 fish bouillon cube and 1 cup of water; add extra water if the recipe calls for a more diluted stock.

BROCCOLI, CHINESE

Called *gai lan* in Chinese, they are leafy greens with tiny white flowers, and despite the name, they don't resemble Western broccoli too much. When cooked, their stems are tender and have a wonderful bittersweet taste. Use regular broccoli if Chinese is not available.

CABBAGE

There are two common varieties, the Chinese or napa cabbage, which is short, and the Japanese, which is tall. Both have sweet, pale stalks with ruffled light green edges and are wonderful in soups and braising dishes. They require less cooking time than Western cabbages.

CHAR SIU SAUCE

See Sauces

CHESTNUTS, DRIED

When fresh chestnuts are not available, use dried ones. Simply soak them for a few hours (or overnight) to rehydrate before cooking.

CHILES, DRIED

The secret to any fiery hot dish. Use whole chiles or break them into small pieces. Remember that the seeds are even hotter than the skin, so use them in moderation. Always wash your hands after handling chiles. The oil on the chiles could irritate your skin or eyes.

CHILES, FRESH

Most of my recipes call for fresh red chiles or green jalapeño chiles. The degree of hotness is entirely up to you; if you prefer a milder dish, replace the fiery Thai red chiles with serrano, jalapeño, or even milder Anaheim chiles.

CHILE OIL

Used as a flavoring agent as well as a condiment at the dining table, this reddish orange oil adds an extra touch of dried red chile to your food.

CHILE PASTE

A thicker, richer form of chile sauce.

CHINESE BARBECUED PORK

Called *char siu* in Chinese. It is oven-roasted pork and is widely available in most Chinese delicatessens. The sweet, rich taste of *char siu* sauce is a combination of honey, soy sauce, garlic, and spices.

CHINESE BLACK VINEGAR

See Vinegar

CHINESE BROCCOLI

See Broccoli

CHINESE CHIVES

See Garlic Chives

CHINESE EGG NOODLES

See Noodles

CHINESE FIVE-SPICE POWDER

A blend of cinnamon, star anise, cloves, fennel, and Sichuan peppercorns, five-spice powder is a popular seasoning for braised meats, roasts, and barbecued dishes.

CHINESE LONG BEANS

Also called yard-long beans, they are long, thin, and dark green in color. Their crunchy texture and a slightly sweet flavor make yard-long beans a great stir-fry dish with meat, poultry, or seafood.

CHINESE PARSLEY

See Cilantro

CHINESE RICE WINE

See Rice Wine

CHINESE SAUSAGE

Called *lop cheong* in Chinese, these 4- to 6-inch links are made from pork, pork fat, duck, liver, or beef, and are seasoned with salt, sugar, and rice wine. Find them in your

Chinese grocers or delis, either fresh or in vacuum packages. The most common way to prepare them is to place them in the same pot when you are making steamed rice. When your rice is done, so are your sausages.

CHOY SUM

Another popular Chinese leafy green, *choy sum* are also called *bok choy sum* (*see Bok Choy*). They have small yellow flowers (edible) among the leaves. Cook them the same way as bok choy.

CILANTRO

A very popular herb in Asian cooking. In North America, the leaves are called cilantro and the seeds coriander; in Britain, both the fresh leaves and seeds are called coriander. To make it even more interesting, the leaves are sometimes called Chinese parsley. They have a very distinctive and refreshing flavor. They are not to be confused with Italian parsley, however. The seeds of coriander (or more accurately, the dried ripe fruits) have the unique sweet flavors of caraway, lemon, and sage.

CLOUD EAR MUSHROOMS

See Mushrooms

COCONUT

Coconut products (milk and cream) are widely used in Asian curries, stews, and desserts. Coconut water is the liquid inside a fresh coconut. It isn't used for cooking but makes a very cool refreshing drink on a warm day. Coconut milk is available in cans; shake well before using. Coconut cream is the thick rich mixture that rises to the top of the coconut milk can. Desiccated coconut is available both in shredded or flake form, sweetened or unsweetened. I recommend the unsweetened variety unless the recipe specifically calls for the sweetened kind.

COOKING OIL

Peanut oil is a common cooking oil in China and other Asian countries. We like it for its fragrance and complex nutty flavor in our stir-fry and deep-fry dishes. Corn oil or other vegetable oils are good alternatives to peanut oil.

CORIANDER

See Cilantro

CUCUMBER

Mostly cultivated in hothouses, English cucumbers can reach to more than 12 inches in length. They are almost seedless, with a thin, bright green skin. Japanese cucumbers are similar to English ones but they are only 1 inch in diameter and 8 inches in length.

CURRY

Some claimed curry to be the most famous invention in India. This spicy mixture blends cumin, cardamom, coriander, chiles, cinnamon, cloves, turmeric (which gives it its yellow coloring), and tamarind.

DAIKON

A radish originating from Japan, daikon has a crisp white texture and a sweet and peppery taste. It is also called Chinese turnip or Chinese radish. In Chinese cooking, daikon is often used in soups and braised and slow-cooked dishes, the same way that turnips or potatoes are used in Western cooking.

EGG ROLL WRAPPERS

See Wrappers

FENNEL

One of the seasonings that make up Chinese five-spice powder, fennel has a slightly licorice flavor and is best used in soups and stews.

FISH BALLS, FISH CAKES

Make your own or find them at your Chinese market. They are ground fish with seasonings and starch, formed into shapes of balls or cakes. In the market, they are sold precooked, either refrigerated or frozen. Fish balls are to be boiled in stock or water or added to soups, while fish cakes can be fried.

FISH SAUCE

See Sauces

FIVE-SPICE POWDER

See Chinese Five-Spice Powder

GARLIC

Probably the most common seasoning in the world, and certainly no stranger to my recipes. As a rule of thumb, one large clove of garlic makes 1 teaspoon minced garlic. Fried garlic is used often as a garnish; you can find it in jars in your Asian markets.

GARLIC CHIVES

Called *gou choy* in Chinese, they are very popular in Chinese cooking as an ingredient as well as a garnish. Green garlic chives resemble wide, long blades of grass, while yellow garlic chives have shorter, more tender leaves and a milder flavor. Flowering garlic chives have firm stalks and small edible buds on top. They are wonderful in stir-fried or steamed dishes.

GINGER

A must in Chinese cooking, fresh ginger has a smooth, pale golden skin, and a fibrous yellow-green interior that gives out a spicy aroma. Young ginger has a more delicate flavor and is less fibrous. Fresh or young, choose tubers with a firm, heavy body and smooth skin without wrinkles or mold. A ginger slice about 1 inch in diameter and 1/4 inch in width will make roughly 1 teaspoon minced ginger. When young ginger is cooked in a sugar syrup, coated in sugar, and then dried, it is called crystallized ginger. Ginger can also be pickled in brine, then soaked in a sugar-vinegar solution. In Japan, the red version of pickled ginger is slightly sweeter. Preserved ginger is stored in a heavy sugar syrup.

HOISIN SAUCE

See Sauces

JICAMA

Similar to Chinese water chestnuts in their sweetness and crunchy texture, jicama is much larger in size and more fibrous, with a brown skin. Pick those that are firm, well-rounded, and smooth, with no blemishes or mold.

KUNG PAO SAUCE

See Sauces

LEMONGRASS

A very popular herb in Southeast Asia, particularly Thailand and Malaysia. It resembles long pale green onions. It releases an aromatic lemony flavor to any dish. Discard the outer layer of the stalk and use the bottom 6 inches of the lemongrass stem.

LILY BUDS

Gives out a delicate musky-sweet flavor to stir-fry dishes and soups. Lily buds are 2- to 3-inch-long brown strands and are usually sold in the dried form at your Asian grocer.

LONGAN

A small round fruit, longan has a smooth brown shell and a sweet translucent flesh interior very similar to that of lychee. Fresh longans are seasonal, but you can find longans in cans or in crystallized form.

LOP CHEONG

See Chinese Sausage

LOQUAT

Small, strawberry-sized, orange-yellow fruit with sweet, aromatic flesh. Loquats are seasonally available in mild-winter areas or year-round in canned or dried form.

LOTUS

A popular item in Chinese cooking, as nearly all parts of the lotus plant are used. Lotus leaves are used to wrap fillings for steaming rice. Lotus roots look like chains of long, thick sausages that are peeled and sliced to add crunch and texture to soups, braised dishes, and stir-fries. Lotus seeds have a delicate flavor and are often used in sweet desserts. They are available fresh or dried.

LYCHEE

Fresh lychees have a crimson-colored peel that is bumpy and rough to the touch. The interior is succulent, sweet, and refreshing. Fresh lychees are available from early summer to autumn, but canned ones can be found year-round.

MUNG BEANS

See Bean Sprouts

MUSHROOMS, FRESH

Chinese black mushrooms (also known as shiitake mushrooms) are very common in Asian markets. Use them in soups and braised dishes for their rich, smooth, velvety texture. Brown and white button mushrooms are great for stir-fry dishes. For a touch of the exotic, try long-stemmed, tiny-capped enoki mushrooms, or the delicate, shell-shaped oyster mushroom. Finally there are straw mushrooms, which are available fresh almost year-round.

MUSHROOMS, DRIED AND IN CANS

Chinese black (shiitake) mushrooms are more often than not sold in their dried form. Other black fungi that are commonly found in your Asian grocer include cloud ear and wood ear mushrooms. Black fungus resembles leather chips and needs to be rehydrated in warm water before cooking. Straw mushrooms can be found in cans. They have a delicate sweet taste and a firm meaty texture. Drain them well before cooking.

MUSTARD

To make Chinese mustard, simply mix mustard powder with water. It is a hot and pungent table condiment that adds a fiery touch to appetizers and main dishes. If Chinese mustard is not available, use English-style dry mustard.

NAPA CABBAGE

See Cabbage

NOODLES

Dried bean thread noodles are made from mung bean starch. They are called *fun see* in Chinese and come in different lengths and thicknesses. Soak them in warm water for about 15 minutes before cooking. Fresh Chinese egg noodles come in many widths, sizes, and flavors. Fresh rice flour noodles are made from long-grain rice flour. They are soft and white in color. Dried rice stick noodles are stiff and brittle, and they also come in different widths and lengths. Soak before using in soups or stir-fry dishes.

OYSTER SAUCE

See Sauces

PEAS, EDIBLE-POD

Snow peas, also called Chinese pea pods, are flat green pods with a crisp and crunchy texture. They have a delicate sweet taste and are wonderful in soups as well as stir-fry dishes. Sugar snap peas have a similar flavor but their pods are thicker.

PEPPERS, BELL

Both red and green bell peppers have a mild and slightly sweet flavor. Use both for color contrast. They can also be found in yellow, orange, purple, and brown.

PEPPERS, HOT

See Chiles

PLUM SAUCE

See Sauces

POTSTICKER WRAPPERS

See Wrappers

RICE

Categorized by grain and texture. Glutinous rice is a short-grain rice with a soft sticky texture when cooked. Its grains are roundish and pearl-like, and it is used mostly in desserts and stuffings. Long-grain rice cooks up firm and fluffy, so it is ideal for fried rice. Medium-grain rice is very popular in Japan and Korea. It is also the rice that is used in a variety of sushi.

RICE CRUSTS, DRIED

Also called rice cakes, these are dried rice squares that you can find in Asian markets, or, if you prefer, make your own. Use them in the Singing Rice and Seafood Soup (see page 37).

RICE STICK NOODLES, DRIED

See Noodles

RICE VINEGAR

See Vinegar

RICE WINE

Made from fermented glutinous rice and millet, good Chinese rice wine has an amber color and a smooth, velvety body. Shao Hsing (or Shaoxing), near Shanghai in Eastern China, produces some of the best quality rice wines, many of which are aged from 10 to 100 years.

ROCK SUGAR

See Sugar, Rock

SAUCES

Black bean sauce is made from salted black beans, garlic, and hot chiles.

Char siu sauce or **barbecue sauce** is a thick sauce made from fermented soybeans, tomato paste, chile, vinegar, garlic, ginger, and sesame oil.

Curry sauce has all the spices and seasonings of a curry ready in a bottle.

Fish sauce is an all-purpose flavoring sauce from Southeast Asia and the southern part of China. Its pungent flavor (made from soy and fish extracts) adds a complex salty flavor to food.

Hoisin sauce is made from fermented soybeans, vinegar, garlic, sugar, and spices, and has a rich, robust flavor. It is the sauce of choice for Mu Shu Pork and the famous Peking Duck.

Hot pepper sauce is a hot and spicy sauce made from Tabasco peppers, vinegar, and salt.

Kung pao sauce is made from red chiles, sesame oil, soybeans, sweet potato, ginger, garlic, and other spices.

Oyster sauce is a thick, brown sauce made from oyster extracts, sugar, and starch. It has a smoky sweet flavor that makes it an ideal all-purpose stir-fry seasoning. For strict vegetarians use vegetarian oyster sauce.

Plum sauce is made from salted plums, apricots, yams, rice vinegar, and chiles. It is sweet and tart and is often served with roast duck, barbecued dishes, and fried appetizer dishes like spring rolls.

Shrimp sauce, or shrimp paste, is made from salted fermented shrimp. It is thick and pungent and is a common ingredient in Southeast Asian cooking.

Soy is the most common Chinese condiment and flavoring agent. Soy sauce comes in light or dark varieties. Select the right soy as indicated in the recipes. "Lite" or sodium-reduced soy sauce contains about 40 percent less salt.

Stir-fry sauce is a generic name for a combination of soy sauce, rice wine, sugar, sesame oil, garlic, and ginger—in other words, all the seasonings you need in any stir-fry dish.

Sweet and sour sauce is made from vinegar and sugar; chiles, ketchup, and ginger are added in some of the popular versions.

Sweet bean sauce is a combination of fermented soybeans and sugar.

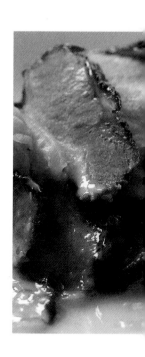

SEAWEED, DRIED

Used mostly in soups in Chinese cooking.

SESAME OIL

Asian sesame oil is extracted by pressing toasted white sesame seeds. High-quality oil carries the label "100 percent pure." Sesame oil is aromatic; a few drops are sufficient to add that nutty taste to marinades, dressings, and stir-fries. Don't use large amounts as a cooking oil.

SESAME SEEDS

White sesame seeds have a sweet, nutty flavor and can be found hulled or unhulled. Black seeds are a little more bitter. Both kinds, often toasted to intensify the aroma, are used to flavor and garnish dishes.

SHAO HSING WINE

See Rice Wine

SHIITAKE MUSHROOMS

See Mushrooms

SHRIMP, DRIED

Dried shrimp are tiny shrimps that are preserved in brine and dried afterwards. They have a chewy texture and a rather pungent taste. Use them in soups and vegetable dishes, as well as dumpling fillings.

SHRIMP, FRESH OR FROZEN

Note size suggestion in recipes since shrimp come in many different sizes.

SICHUAN PEPPERCORNS

Reddish-brown in color, these "peppercorns" are actually berries from the prickly ash tree. They add a woodsy fragrance to food. Their flavors intensify when you toast them in a frying pan over medium heat. Once toasted, use either whole peppercorns or grind them into a fine powder.

SICHUAN PRESERVED VEGETABLE

Chinese mustard greens, napa cabbage, and turnips are preserved in salt, ground chile, and ground Sichuan peppercorns to give them a spicy and salty taste.

SNOW PEAS

See Peas, Edible-Pod

SOYBEANS

High in vegetable protein and other nutrients, soybeans can be eaten steamed and are the base for a wide variety of Chinese food products, such as soy sauce, tofu, bean sprouts, bean curd sheets, pressed bean curds, soybean oil, and soybean paste.

SOY SAUCE

See Sauces

SPRING ROLL WRAPPERS

See Wrappers

STAR ANISE

A hard, eight-pointed star pod encasing small seeds that is used to give a spicy licorice flavor to braising sauces and stews. Use broken points if whole pods are not available.

STRAW MUSHROOMS

See Mushrooms

SUGAR, ROCK

Hard, pale amber-colored crystals, rock sugar is also referred to as rock candy; it is made from a combination of refined and raw sugars and honey. It is best used in braised meat dishes and savory sauces.

SWEET AND SOUR SAUCE

See Sauces

TANGERINE PEEL, DRIED

Dried tangerine peel adds a wonderful citrus flavor to sauces, soups, and braised dishes. Rehydrate the hard, rust-brown peel in warm water until softened before use. You can find dried tangerine peel in your Asian grocer or you may make your own by drying the skin in the sun or in a cool oven. Once dried, store in an air-tight container.

TAPIOCA

Tapioca starch is made from the root of cassava plants. It is a common thickening agent. It is also combined with other flours to make dim sum. Tapioca pearls are tiny beads of tapioca that are used in creamy puddings and other sweet desserts.

TOFU

Also referred to as soybean curd, tofu is made from soybeans and water. Tofu is categorized by its firmness, from silky and soft to firm. The softer the tofu, the higher the water content remains inside the curd. Fermented tofu has a pungent wine-like aroma and the consistency of thick custard; it is used most often in claypot and braised dishes. For spice lovers, there is spicy red fermented tofu. Pressed tofu has a firm texture, which means most of the water has been removed. It comes in regular or spicy flavor. Many nutritionists recommend pressed tofu as a meat substitute for its texture and high protein content. Fresh or dried bean curd sheets are thin sheets made out of tofu and are used most often in soups and claypot dishes.

VINEGAR

Chinese black vinegar is made by fermenting a mixture of rice, wheat, and millet or sorghum. It has a smoky, somewhat sweet flavor when compared to regular white distilled vinegar, which is more tart and lighter in body. A popular black vinegar is Chinkiang vinegar, produced in Eastern China near Shanghai. If black vinegar is not available, use balsamic vinegar and decrease the sugar content in the recipe to compensate for the sweeter nature of balsamic. Rice vinegar is made from fermented rice; it is not as acidic and pungent as black vinegar, but sweeter than white vinegar.

WATER CHESTNUTS

Fresh water chestnuts are small round tubers with a brown skin and sweet crunchy white flesh. Pick ones that are firm, and free of wrinkles and mold. They must be peeled before using. Water chestnuts also come ready peeled in cans, but are not as sweet and should be rinsed before using in salads or other dishes.

WINE, CHINESE RICE

See Rice Wine

WOOD EAR MUSHROOMS

See Mushrooms

WRAPPERS

Egg roll wrappers are thin, square sheets made from wheat flour, eggs, and water. They are similar to wonton wrappers in texture but are larger in size and, once filled with either a savory or sweet filling, are deep-fried. Wonton wrappers come in two thicknesses; the thick ones are for deep-frying, pan-frying, or steaming, while the thin ones are best in soups. Potsticker wrappers are circles cut from a similar dough and can be fried or steamed. Spring roll wrappers are thinner than egg roll wrappers; they are made of wheat flour and water, which gives them a lighter, crispier texture when they are deep-fried.

YARD-LONG BEANS

See Chinese Long Beans

INDEX

ACKNOWLEDGMENTS

I learned a long time ago that a successful chef does not work alone. Behind every successful master chef is a well-managed and well-organized kitchen. The same can be said about any successful cookbook author. Behind each one of them is a talented and highly dedicated supporting staff. Over the years, I have had the great privilege to work with one of the most talented culinary teams anywhere. *Martin Yan's Invitation to Chinese Cooking* is the latest fruit of their collective labor.

My thanks must first go to Tina Salter, who pioneered this project and worked relentlessly to assure its high production quality and timely completion. My thanks also go to my editor, Clare Johnson of Pavilion Books, for her professional expertise, patience, advice, and support.

A cookbook is much more than a collection of recipes. I want to thank Janet James for a most beautiful design and layout, and James Murphy, Allyson Birch, and Helene Lesur for doing great photographic justice to the recipes. Thanks must also go to Ivan Lai, Jennifer Louie, Margaret McKinnon, Jan Nix, Ann Ny Matsuda, and Sandra Rust for their long hours of research and contribution to the text.

Assuring each ingredient in each of my recipes is exactly right is the responsibility of my dedicated recipe testing staff—Bernice C. Fong, Stephanie Jan, Winnie Lee, Jan Nix, Carol Odman, Frankie Poon, and Sandra Rust. Thank you, gang, another job well done!

Last but certainly not least, my thanks must go out to all of you, my television fans and readers, for bestowing me honor by selecting this book. I hope you will enjoy *Martin Yan's Invitation to Chinese Cooking*, and I shall look forward to cooking along with you again in many of your future culinary adventures.

ABOUT MARTIN YAN

Martin Yan, celebrated host of more than 1,500 cooking shows in the U.S., highly respected food and restaurant consultant, and certified Master Chef, enjoys distinction as both teacher and author. His many talents have found unique expression in numerous cookbooks, including *Martin Yan's Feast, Martin Yan's Asia,* and *Martin Yan's Culinary Journey Through China.*

Born in Guangzhou, China, Yan always possessed a passion for cooking. His formal introduction to the culinary world started at thirteen when he began his first apprenticeship for a well-established Hong Kong restaurant. After earning his diploma from the Overseas Institute of Cookery, Hong Kong, he traveled to Canada and then on to California.

Before receiving his M.S. in Food Science from the University of California, Davis, in 1975, Yan taught Chinese cooking for the University of California extension program. He later moved back to Canada and soon became the well-known and much loved host of the syndicated show *Yan Can Cook*. He has been a guest chef and instructor at many professional chef programs, including the California Culinary Academy and Johnson & Wales University (he serves on both schools' advisory committees), the University of San Francisco, and Chinese chef training programs across North America. Yan is the founder of the Yan Can International Cooking School in Foster City, California.

Today, Martin Yan enjoys national and international recognition among his peers as a master chef.

Yan Can Cook was twice recognized by the James Beard Foundation with the James Beard Award for Best Television Cooking Show in 1994 and Best Television Food Journalism in 1996. Yan has also been honored with the prestigious Antonin Carême Award by the Chef's Association of the Pacific Coast and the Courvoisier Leadership Award. Along with Paul Prudhomme, he was named Culinary Diplomat for the American Culinary Federation, and in recognition of his contribution to the food and hospitality industry he received—along with America's First Lady of cooking, Julia Child—an Honorary Degree in Culinary Arts from the leading culinary training mecca, Johnson & Wales University.

Yan has captured the admiration and loyal following of thousands of *Yan Can Cook* fans by combining his cooking artistry and teaching skill with a most personal and unique ingredient: humor. His cooking demonstrations, on television or in person, are as entertaining as they are educational. He is dedicated to dispelling the mysteries of Asian cooking and furthering the understanding and enjoyment of the cuisines of Asia.